Good Tidings
and
Great Joy

ALSO BY SARAH PALIN

Going Rogue

America by Heart

Good Tidings
and
Great Joy

Protecting the Heart of Christmas

Sarah Palin

HARPER LUXE

An Imprint of HarperCollins*Publishers*

GOOD TIDINGS AND GREAT JOY. Copyright © 2013 by Sarah Palin. All rights reserved. Printed in the United States of America. No part of this book may be used or reproduced in any manner whatsoever without written permission except in the case of brief quotations embodied in critical articles and reviews. For information address HarperCollins Publishers, 10 East 53rd Street, New York, NY 10022.

HarperCollins books may be purchased for educational, business, or sales promotional use. For information, please e-mail the Special Markets Department at SPsales@harpercollins.com.

FIRST HARPERLUXE EDITION

HarperLuxe™ is a trademark of HarperCollins Publishers

Library of Congress Cataloging-in-Publication Data is available upon request.

ISBN: 978-0-06-229789-1

13 14 ID/RRD 10 9 8 7 6 5 4 3 2 1

To Mom and Dad.
Thank you for the most unique and inspiring upbringing. You taught us to work very hard and to fight for what's right. From you I learned to lean into the exhaustion of hard work, which turns out to be exhilarating.

And it's fun to watch you live like every day is Christmas.

Our world needs more of that.

All this for *me*? And I wasn't even very good!

—*My grandson,* TRIPP EASTON MITCHELL,
*upon seeing the presents beneath
the Christmas tree, 2012*

My dad, my aunt Carol, and my
grandmother Marie in 1944, when they
lived in North Hollywood.

Contents

Good Tidings
and
Great Joy

I remember one present specifically from
Christmas 1968 in our tiny Gold Rush town
of Skagway, Alaska—this sweet teddy bear,
which I kept for years.

Introduction

I've never had to dream of a white Christmas.

Growing up in Alaska, I didn't have to imagine snow. It wasn't some romantic notion or a fluffy excuse to get out of school. It was something I shoveled from the driveway, threw at my brother, and ate with my sisters. I never thought of snow as a picturesque backdrop for Christmas cards that would politely melt away for safer New Year's Eve parties. Our snow seemed relentless, heavy, and sometimes even threatening—a force to be reckoned with, an ever-present reality that stole the sure footing on roadways, caused roofs to collapse, and made us children squeal in delight.

Though we were always guaranteed a "white Christmas," the magic of the Last Frontier reached far beyond the stunning, icy backdrop. I grew up just three hundred miles from North Pole, Alaska. Okay, it isn't the *true* North Pole, but don't tell that to the hundreds of thousands of children who've sent letters there over the years. Alaska is the perfect place to watch for Santa and his reindeer, as the spectacular northern lights make them easier to spot. There's something about the harsh, cold outdoors that makes opening Christmas presents by the fireplace so cozy.

Like many Americans, we have fun, long-standing family Christmas traditions. For years, we cut down our tree from our own, or friends', property. We plop the sometimes Charlie Brown–looking spruce in our living room, tether it with fish line, and decorate it with our variety of ornaments collected over the years: fat Santas, comically slender snowmen, pine-cones topped with velvet ribbons, sticky sweet candy canes, and felt mittens with the kids' lopsided names written on the backs in Sharpie markers. Oh, and we bake. Usually, my sisters, mom, daughters, and best girlfriends join me in the kitchen, and we bake until the smell of cinnamon rolls overtakes the aroma of our Alaska spruce.

We live out the old song, "over the river and through the woods to grandmother's house we go," but with a more efficient method of travel. On icy Christmas Eves and that climactic next morning, we often jump on our snowmachines and wind our way around frozen natural trail markers and under the snow-covered branches of the cottonwood trees. One by one, we make our way through the woods and along the roadside, as gorgeous white powder kicks up around us and the frigid air bites any exposed skin on our faces. We glide through our valley embraced by majestic mountains with my family, occasionally startling a moose, passing caribou farther north, and hoping the kids in the back keep up. As governor, I was able to see even more jaw-dropping vistas throughout Alaska. But the most beautiful scenes were the ones I've taken in through the lenses of my snowmachine goggles.

When we arrive at the homes of our friends and families, we frequently play Eskimo Bingo, a gift-swapping game and the only time we enthusiastically encourage the kids to be greedy. Everyone brings a wrapped gift for exchange and places it on the floor. With a timer ticking, we roll dice in a pie tin and hope to get doubles so the gift-grabbing can begin. Each person gets to "steal" presents from the center of our circle, even ones already nabbed. This might sound like a fun parlor game, but it gets intense. When someone unwraps something good and places it on the floor, even for a moment, it's fair game. One year, a highly coveted box of homemade chocolates from a bakery in

Indiana caused us to play well into the night. (I ended up with that one because I'm the mom, and I refused to let the game end until it ended well.) Some years, I've ended up with one of the gag gifts—a singing-fish wall plaque, a dusty old fossil from Dad's garage shelf, a warped tin sign that reads, GIVE ME A BEER, THE IN-LAWS ARE HERE.

But Todd makes sure my real Christmas gifts are amazing.

He's always given good gifts.

When we were seventeen—and my friends had already received Polo sweaters, the newest Go-Gos vinyl record, or Gloria Vanderbilt jeans from their boyfriends—Todd surprised me with a traditional Eskimo grass-woven basket and Alaska gold nugget earrings from a native village near his hometown. In that tradition, he has since given me a beautiful red manual ice auger for ice fishing on the lake, a .30-06 rifle, a pair of hockey skates, snowshoes for hard-core winter workouts, and cords of seasoned spruce for my fireplace. (I so appreciate that one, as I have an unusual affinity for chopping and stacking my own wood. As the old saying goes: "Chop your own wood and it'll warm you twice.") No Christmas lilies or lavender bubble bath in the stocking from this dude, no sir. He's as unique as his gifts. I've tried to reciprocate with thoughtful presents, but all Todd wants is the same thing: gift cards for gas to keep his snowmachine, truck, and float plane topped off. Ahhh, I love that he's easy to please.

Last year, however, I think I was able to pull off a good one for him. To combat the anti-gun chatter coming from Washington, I surprised him with a nice, needed, powerful gun. I then asked him for a metal gun holder for my four-wheeler. Not only was this small act of civil disobedience fun, it allowed me to finally live out one of my favorite lines from a country song: "He's got the rifle, I got the rack."

But it goes without saying that one of the most enjoyable parts of Christmas has always been giving gifts to the children. There's nothing like watching their sleepy eyes turn wide when they see the presents under the tree. When Track and Bristol were little, I was overflowing with energy and all those "new mom ideas," so I decided to lead them to their gifts gradually by creating Christmas scavenger hunts. I'd give them the first clue in their stockings, which would lead them to the second clue, which would lead them to the third. It was delightful to see their growing anticipation as they got closer to their "big present," which might have been a BB gun, a doll, or the perfect lunch box (anything besides new underwear and more wool socks). Yes, the scavenger hunt added a little adventure to an already amazing day.

Would you believe that more than twenty years later, this tradition still lives on in the Palin household? Even though the kids are now receiving electronics and clothes instead of Hot Wheels, I still create a labyrinth of clues for the Christmas-morning gift hunts. I love tradition, but I have to admit: It's kicking my butt. I've hidden clues in every cookie jar, out in the woodpile, on the gate, under chunks of wild game in the freezer, on the truck's trailer hitch, and even on the dog's collar. Not only have I run out of good hiding places, but I'm sure the kids are absolutely annoyed they still have to spend those cold, cold Christmas mornings searching high and low for their next clue. So I ask myself, *Can't I just please stay in my pajamas, sip hot coffee, and look out over Lake Lucille while the kids open their presents in front of the warm fireplace, please?* But mom guilt nudges me awake at dawn to hide clues in bird feeders and bathtubs, so I can keep the magic alive at least one more year.

And this gets to the heart of it, doesn't it? These Christmases are more fragile than I want to admit. Since Todd and I first began our life together, so much has happened. We've experienced five babies, countless scraped knees and stitches, twenty Iron Dog races, seven political campaigns, two tear-filled Army deployments and safe returns, one vice-presidential run, two amazing grandchildren, more than one ridiculous magazine cover, and a few bumps in the road along the way. It's a miracle what families can endure, and I've always appreciated our ability to stick together through the toughest of times. It seems inherent and perfectly appropriate that families do "circle the wagon" in challenging times. No matter what, my family will always do Christmas together.

But while our family has worked hard to hold tight to our Christmas traditions, I wonder just how easy it will be in the future to joyfully and openly celebrate. Christmas has come under attack in recent years, and it's not just some figment of the religious right's imagination. I think of this every time I see a news story about an ACLU letter warning a school district not to sing "Silent Night," or when a college group isn't permitted to advertise a Christmas tree sale, or when "Merry Christmas" is replaced by the more politically correct "Happy Holidays"—all to avoid giving offense. I'm concerned that the years of relentless attacks against the holiday will eventually drain the joy from our public spaces as well as from our minds and hearts.

Our cultural elites have even gone out of their way to create legal doctrines that allow "offended observers" to file lawsuits against public religious displays, like Nativity scenes—even though in virtually no other area of law does a person have a right to go to court merely because they are "offended" by something a school or a town does. These same elites often treat these thin-skinned, litigious citizens as cultural heroes—fighting against a tradition they despise—while they laugh at folks offended when symbols of our cultural heritage are stripped from the public square.

They send us the message that "Christmas" is something best practiced at home, as if it's a shameful and potentially exclusionary personal lifestyle choice. Perhaps Christmas causes so much anger because the very name of the holiday broadcasts the Name above all Names. Our annual family activities I've described are mere traditions . . . little rituals that amuse, sometimes irritate, mostly delight, and endure year after year. But they'd be nothing if separated from the historical event that animates the Christmas season—the event that gives our hearts the joy to celebrate: the birth of Jesus.

There are two competing visions of December 25. One recognizes that the birth of Christ was one of the most significant moments in world history. More than just a historical event, the arrival of Jesus on earth was the first step toward atonement, redemption, and resurrection. He was "God made flesh," the true hope of the world.

If I'm for Christmas, it's only because I'm for Christ.

The other vision is a secular winter festival, which launches on Black Friday and ends sometime after Kwanzaa. People who hold Christmas in contempt believe the holiday can be "saved" from its religious heritage. The secular vision wants the "peace" and "goodwill toward men" without the miracle of the Virgin Birth—forgetting, of course, that there is no ultimate peace apart from Christ, and it is Christ who empowers every act of "goodwill toward men" in our otherwise fallen hearts.

The pundits like to pretend that anyone who belongs to the "Christmas with Christ" version is picking a fight over a nonexistent problem. They trivialize the topic by reducing the whole issue to whether the cashier at the grocery store wishes customers "Merry Christmas" or "Happy Holidays." They say it's about whether the kids' two weeks off in December is called Winter or Christmas Break. They argue "Jingle Bells" is more catchy than the tired old "Silent Night." (Plus, it won't run the risk of offending the atheist couple in the eleventh row.) They claim the whole conversation is the result of hypersensitivity, intolerance, or—their favorite criticism for us "bitter clingers"—ignorance and fear of change. (See how I did that? I just summarized 90 percent of the book reviews for my critics, so they don't even have to read the rest. You betcha, I helped you out!)

But let me tell you why this conversation is important.

This book is not about isolated trivialities. It's not really about gingerbread cookies, or stockings hung by the chimney with care, or the big fat man with the long white beard. It's not about a holiday at all. It's about that little baby wrapped in swaddling clothes, who arrived long before hope and change became political manipulations. It's about Christ and our ability to worship Him freely. It's about America, and what liberty truly means in our day-to-day lives.

The battle for Christmas is more significant than the sneering media will lead you to believe. Boiled down to its essence, the "war on Christmas" is the tip of the spear in a larger battle to secularize our culture and make true religious freedom a thing of America's past. Far from a hand-wringing tale of woe, however, this book is a story of hope and a plan to protect our holiday heritage.

It may just change your life.

There is something that happens deep within you when you realize that you don't have to be intimidated by the political correctness police. You can live a life of faith, stand tall against the finger-wagging intolerants who want to fundamentally transform our country, and protect our heritage while living out the values that made this nation exceptional.

But first, let's take a closer look at the problem and the people trying to secularize the season.

Let's call them the Scrooges.

Chuck Jr., Heather, and I anticipate opening
presents in Skagway, Alaska, in 1968.
Though the tree looks Charlie Brown–ish
here, it was actually very pretty!

1

Angry Atheists with Lawyers

In the old days, it was not called the Holiday Season; the Christians called it "Christmas" and went to church; the Jews called it "Hanukka" and went to synagogue; the atheists went to parties and drank. People passing each other on the street would say "Merry Christmas!" or "Happy Hanukka!" or (to the atheists) "Look out for the wall!"

—DAVE BARRY

It was a perfectly crisp December 25, 1978, and we'd already opened our presents, devoured an early turkey dinner, and gulped our hot chocolate. Dad and Mom were cleaning up the wonderful Christmas clutter off our living room's green shag carpet.

"Go enjoy the sun," Mom said, in the way only an Alaska mother would. It was probably in the low teens temperature-wise; the sun had come out of its hiding but was already aiming to dip below the horizon. During those long, dark winters, the days are so brief they're too easy to miss entirely, because the sun rises and sets within about five hours. We didn't want Christmas day—of all days—to slip by.

"Grab the wrench!" I yelled to my brother as I ran out the door. We hopped on our old snowmachine, which only responded to whacks of a wrench that would wiggle spark plugs magically enough to restart the cold engine. We wound through our town on that ancient Polaris we shared, and the frigid air bit my nose.

Suddenly, my brother pulled the machine to a complete stop.

"What are you doing?" I asked him, impatiently. But just then, I turned around and saw a tall, glaring state trooper. He had a badge and a gun, and a chill, unrelated to the temperature, went straight through me.

"What are you kids up to?" he growled.

There couldn't have been more than a couple of troopers in our sparsely populated area, which is physically huge—our borough is about the size of the state of West Virginia—but, just our luck, we found one on Christmas morning. Rather, he found us. After a discussion wherein we convinced the officer we were really "not up to no good," he let us go. When we drove off, I was stewing. That officer didn't have one ounce of Christmas cheer.

We've all run into those who don't quite seem to have the joy of the season in their hearts and minds—at the mall when there are too few parking spaces for last-minute shoppers, at the office party when someone has too much eggnog, at home when the kids eat all the decorated chocolate peanut butter balls you wrapped for neighbors, or at the in-laws' when the toddler finally smashes the shiny glass tree ornaments. We've all—at times—lost sight of the true meaning of the season. But there are many people who haven't merely lost, misplaced, or forgotten the true meaning of Christmas, they're trying to actively target it to destroy it. And these true Scrooges have a frightening amount of power.

This modern-day Scrooge—let's call him "Joe McScrooge" for short—threatens to destroy every last bit of Christmas cheer we have left.

Let me set the scene:

It was too cold, the wind was too strong, and his rental car smelled vaguely of cigarette smoke. His plane had been thirty minutes late, and Joe

McScrooge was angry. While he waited for his car to heat up, he turned on the satellite radio, which was thankfully already tuned to NPR. The host was interviewing a man who was helping under-privileged children overcome their religious super-stition, intolerance, and bullying tendencies.

He glanced at the clock: 6:35. The airport was at least twenty minutes from Benjamin Franklin Elementary School, according to his GPS, so he had no time to waste to get to his son's Winter program.

It was his first visit to this small Pennsylvania town since his ex-wife gained custody and moved almost two thousand miles away from the warm sands of New Mexico. He turned up the radio and listened to the host's calming voice. He needed to hear some reasonable conversation before the forced sentimentality of the school program.

It was dusk, but he could still check out the town through the glass of his windshield. Shabby. Low-class. A strip mall here, a strip mall there—no ap-parent zoning rules or urban planning. And, of course, there it was, the inevitable Wal-Mart Supercenter. He snorted to himself as he passed a fast-food restaurant with a sign that read,

JESUS IS THE REASON FOR THE SEASON

What the heck does religion have to do with french fries?

At a stop sign, a man walked his huge unpedigreed dog in front of Joe's car into a small park that had a sign:

PRIVATE RYAN REYNOLDS CITY PARK

There, across the field, out of the corner of his eye, he noticed a cross next to a statue of a soldier kneeling in prayer. His grip tightened on the steering wheel. "As if only Christians have died for their country," he said to himself as he watched the sweaterless dog shake free of his master's grip on the leash. "Our wars aren't holy wars, our soldiers aren't holy men, and that's a government park."

He pushed it from his mind as he drove into the center of town. Wreaths were hanging from every storefront. Christmas lights wrapped around the light poles were blinking relentlessly. Red ribbons flapped sloppily in the breeze, Joe noticed. The lights were multicolored and garish, and Joe was annoyed at their distraction. As he drove closer to the court square, however, his jaw dropped.

There, right next to the courthouse—between a metal newspaper box and a ridiculously oversized menorah—was the unmistakable outline of a Nativity scene. It included the baby Jesus, the "virgin" Mary, and her gullible fiancé, Joseph. The only miracle in that story was the fact that Joseph apparently fell for Mary's story of a divine insemination.

The Bible's no better than The Jerry Springer Show, Joe thought. How on earth do these people believe such drivel? He took the turn slowly, checking out the cheap plastic baby Jesus doll nestled in hay.

He could almost feel his blood pressure rise. The doctor had warned him. "Avoid stress," he had said. "Stay away from difficult situations." Joe actually laughed out loud as he remembered that conversation in the doctor's office. He was going to see his son for the first time in six months, visit with his ex-wife, and meet her new boyfriend. That was stressful enough.

"Now I have to be reminded I'm an outsider in my own country?"

He took one last glance at the public display, and mumbled to himself, "Namaste," as he drove through the town.

The school parking lot was almost full, and he had to drive near the football stadium, weaving through minivans and SUVs. He parked between two pickup trucks, one sporting a red-and-gold Semper Fi window decal, the other a faded, peeling McCain/Palin '08 bumper sticker. Joe audibly gagged. As he walked by the older buildings, he noticed the school wasn't as new and shiny as the more modern Cesar Chavez School his son used to attend. Before his ex-wife got custody and moved to this dump of a town. The school's sign read, in slightly crooked black letters:

CHRISTMAS BREAK: DECEMBER 19TH THROUGH 25TH. HAVE A MERRY CHRISTMAS.

"Do only Christians attend this school?" he asked the teenage girl handing out programs.

"Excuse me?" she asked, smiling through her braces and fumbling with her WELCOME. MY NAME IS: REBECCA name tag. Joe reminded himself that it wasn't her fault. She was just a kid. He doubted that school even taught about the separation of church and state.

"Never mind," he said, taking the program and hoping he wouldn't run into his ex before the show started.

"Merry Christmas," Rebecca chirped as he walked away.

He stopped in his tracks, turned around slowly, and curtly responded, "A happy holiday to you, too." She smiled and continued to hand out programs, completely oblivious to how insensitive she was acting. He found a seat in the back row and tried to relax. But when he opened the program and glanced over the songs, his hands began to tremble. Three of the ten songs were definitely religious carols: "Silent Night," "Joy to the World," and "Little Drummer Boy." He exhaled to calm his nerves. He couldn't shake the feeling that he was back in that old dusty church of his childhood. When the lights finally went down, the principal bounded up the steps and strode across the stage. She was slightly overweight, Joe couldn't help but notice, and her goofy green reindeer-adorned sweater looked as shabby as the rest of the town.

"Merry Christmas, everyone," she sang. "Thank you so much for coming out on this cold night for our program." As soon as her religion-specific greeting faded from the echo of the cheap public-address system, children standing on bleachers began singing the most dreary of all songs: "Silent Night." Joe plastered a smile on his face, and scanned the rows of children to find his son. They all looked the same from his back-row seat. Finally, his eyes focused on his boy, and he found himself scooting forward and waving and grinning at him in spite of his bad mood. His son looked taller than he remembered, and so handsome standing there in the second row, fifth young man from the left. Joe could tell his son was singing the words happily, not even realizing the offensive silliness of the whole production.

At that, all his joy faded.

Joe sighed, got out his iPhone, and tried to shield its glow with his hand. "You seriously won't believe where I am," he tapped out on his phone. He hadn't talked to his lawyer since the divorce proceedings, but he knew he'd get a kick out of this one. "I've seen more constitutional violations with my own eyes in just the past hour than a prison guard at Abu Ghraib." He pressed send, slid the phone into his pocket, and tried to focus. The children had thankfully transitioned to "Rudolph the Red-Nosed Reindeer." Still ridiculous, but not as . . . well, illegal. He couldn't believe he'd come all this way just to be marginalized. He'd been marginalized in his family, and now he'd been marginalized by his country.

Just a few seconds later, his phone beeped. Joe ran his hands over the side to turn off the volume. The text was from his lawyer, and it simply said:

I'm curious. Let's talk tomorrow.

You might think Joe's story is a far-fetched stereotype, that no one could ever actually be as thin-skinned as poor Mr. McScrooge. You might even feel a little sympathy for the guy, because he holds viewpoints obviously outside the mainstream; he feels isolated and that his views aren't adequately expressed—even though seven out of the ten songs in his kid's program were profoundly secular.

But while "Joe McScrooge" himself is a made-up character, there are actually many such Scrooges all over America. They're very angry, and—thanks to a highly technical quirk in constitutional law very few people know about and even fewer understand—they are very, very influential. An angry atheist with a lawyer is one of the most powerful persons in America.

Why?

To understand this phenomenon, you have to know just a little bit about the law: about why and how you can file a lawsuit, about why and how your rights are normally protected, about why and who can sue a city, county, or school.

Normally, a person can't sue a public entity for a violation of constitutional rights unless he or she has a concrete injury. Someone would have to show how the action of the public institution harmed his legally protected interests. For example, if you're told not to speak, your right to free speech has been violated. If you're censored, the government has deprived you of your ability to express yourself. If the police enter your home without a search warrant, your right to be free from an unreasonable search and seizure has been violated. If you're prohibited from holding a Bible study, your right to free exercise of religion has been compromised. In all of these examples, the power of the state is forcing you into silence or subjection.

Traditionally, however, Americans don't have a right to not be offended—being offended is not an "injury" the law recognizes. You can't sue because you have been exposed to contrary viewpoints—even angry or vicious viewpoints, which are just a part of living in a vibrant democracy. Nowhere is this more apparent than in the presidential elections, which I had the privilege of seeing up close and personal in 2008. During that campaign, I saw obscene protesters, had my personal e-mail account hacked, was mischaracterized through ridiculously scandalous headlines, received death threats, and was stalked. We experienced more concentrated "offense" than anyone could have dreamed, but it was all part of a democratic process of electing new leaders for this great country.

Even on the local level, you can't expect to agree with your neighbor and he can't necessarily expect to agree with you. Imagine what a boring world it would be if everyone always agreed on everything. Or, worse, imagine what would happen if disagreements in viewpoints provided enough cause to file suits. Discussions at the local coffee shop and even arguments in the public square make us think about issues in different ways and sometimes even make us change our minds.

The government can irritate you in many ways—especially when you didn't vote for the guy who won the last election—without violating your rights. When that happens, you can speak out against its actions, vote against a political leader, or campaign for someone who can enact better policies. What you can't do is sue the government just because you felt offended. Otherwise our courts would be flooded with lawsuits every time a legislator says something stupid on the House floor, or when a teacher advances a personal viewpoint that students or parents don't like, or when a mayor insults his constituents during a television interview.

Barack Obama, for example, didn't face 60 million lawsuits when he repeatedly implied that fiscally concerned and conservative Americans care more about tax breaks for the rich than for the well-being of poor citizens. That's a very offensive sentiment indeed, expressed by the most powerful man on earth. It's obvious that the statement was explicitly designed to make almost half the country feel like outsiders. But the fact that we're offended—even when he means to offend—doesn't give us a right to sue. But we can speak out against the president, argue against his policies, and—in the next election—vote for a less offensive candidate.

Everything I've said about our right not to be offended is true.

Except.

Here's the quirk.

If someone is offended by a religious expression or speech in a public setting, then courts have allowed that offended person to sue . . . even if they weren't censored, made to pray, or coerced into compliance with a different belief system, and even when they have a right to speak out and try to change public policy. Not only can people sue over hurt feelings—many times they've won. This means people can silence their fellow citizens for no other reason than the fact that they were offended.

Let's take Joe from our previous example. He didn't have to stare at the Nativity scene, nor did he have to stay and listen to the carols he didn't want to hear at the Christmas program. He could have plopped in some earbuds, listened to his NPR app, walked out, or even written a blog post about how inane he found the elementary school program. No one forced him to do anything. However, because of this strange quirk of the law—a quirk intentionally designed to enable people to complain and remove expressions of our religious heritage from public life—Mr. McScrooge is a legal force to be reckoned with.

In his story, he encountered the cross at the memorial park, the Nativity scene at the courthouse, and the carols at an elementary school Christmas program. I purposely selected these events, because they are examples—as they say—yanked from the headlines. Ready to look at the real cases? You might want to sit down for this.

THE CROSS

There are few things that anger a secular liberal atheist more than a horizontal plank intersecting a vertical plank—a cross—on public land. Perhaps the most extreme example of this is the effort of atheists to remove from the 9/11 Memorial and Museum a cross that provided comfort and solace to many Americans after the September 11, 2001, terrorist attacks.

You may remember this story. It was such a dark time in our history that the news channels were looking desperately for good news, as selfless rescuers were digging for any survivors. Two days after the atrocious terrorist attacks, a worker named Frank Silecchia was busy cutting through the tangled, warped steel beams of the fallen towers. The dust was so thick, it was like snow. He often looked back at the trail he left behind. Even though he was exhausted from the work, he grabbed some gloves, a bottle of water, and a flashlight, and headed into what was left of Building 6. There was so much darkness and devastation around him, he didn't see it at first. Then, he looked down and he saw two steel beams, probably from the North Tower, still connected in the shape of a cross.

"I was so overcome with the sight of the cross that it brought me to my knees in tears. Because I was taken by the whole experience, seeing the devastation of the Trade Center and seeing my country attacked . . . it revitalized me," he said. "It allowed me to persevere. . . . It was one of the most beautiful sights I ever saw."

Immediately reporters, eager for some sort of good news, broadcast photos of this amazing cross. Workers who had access to the site gathered around it to pray, to cry, to search for answers. The Ground Zero cross was a physical part of the story of that dreadful attack, forever a part of our history.

When the curators of the 9/11 museum decided to include this cross in its display of the World Trade Center artifacts, however, American Atheists filed a lawsuit. In their filing, they claimed the cross had no business being in the museum, that its inclusion violated the Constitution, and—get this—some atheists got physically and mentally ill at its mere existence. Their lawsuit, *American Atheists v. Port Authority of New York and New Jersey*, provides some pretty amusing reading:

> *The plaintiffs, and each of them, are suffering, and will continue to suffer damages, both physical and emotional, from the existence of the challenged cross.*

and

> *Named plaintiffs have suffered . . . dyspepsia, symptoms of depression, headaches, anxiety, and mental pain and anguish from the knowledge that they are made to feel officially excluded from the*

ranks of citizens who were directly injured by the 9/11 attack.

The mere thought of the cross in the museum makes them sick? That sounds more like vampires in Transylvania than hearty and hardy citizens of the United States of America.

Not only did they try to remove the cross, they themselves went out of their way to be offensive to faithful Americans. The president of their organization, David Silverman, said: "The World Trade Center cross has become a Christian icon. It has been blessed by so-called holy men and presented as a reminder that their God, who couldn't be bothered to stop the terrorists or prevent 3,000 people from being killed in his name, cared only enough to bestow upon us some rubble that resembles a cross."

So much for not wanting anyone to be offended.

Now, imagine for a moment the hysterical laughter that would ensue in the Lamestream Media if people from a pro-family group filed a lawsuit against the news networks claiming that, for example, the shot of Roseanne Barr grabbing her crotch while screeching and spitting through our national anthem at a Padres game made them physically ill. Or imagine what would happen if Christian parents filed a lawsuit against a public school because their children felt nauseated every time the teacher referred to "Mother Nature" instead of God in their Earth Day materials. The media, of course, would treat those types of lawsuits with utter contempt. They'd characterize the plaintiffs as religious nutcases, too soft and weak-willed to handle a pluralistic society. Yet, the American Atheists were treated with respect as the LSM dutifully reported on their efforts to remove Christ—or even the memory of the steel cross of 9/11—from the public square. Unfortunately this is not the only example of cross displays being challenged.

In the 1930s, the Veterans of Foreign Wars put up a cross in the Mojave Desert—in an isolated area known as Sunrise Rock—to honor our brave soldiers who died in World War I. The modest cross, made out of eight-foot metal pipes painted white, sat on 1.6 acres of desert, 90 percent of which is federal land. Though it was "in the middle of nowhere," it meant such a great deal to many people. In 1983, when a World War I veteran lay on his deathbed, he asked his best friend, Henry Sandoz, to take care of the cross. And that's exactly what Henry faithfully did every year after his friend's death.

Henry was in his seventies by the time Frank Buono, helped by the American Civil Liberties Union, filed a lawsuit claiming that this lovingly maintained old cross unconstitutionally promoted the Christian faith. As the case bounced from one court to another, the cross was enclosed with plywood, covered like an adult magazine in the back of a bookstore. Over the course of the court battle, which went all the way to the Supreme Court, it was even stolen. Finally, after eight long years of battling, the cross was able to remain on the land by transferring the property surrounding it to a private citizen.

But not all crosses have survived litigation. The Utah Highway Patrol Association erected fourteen crosses on state land and private property to honor officers who had died in the line of duty. The crosses were placed near the locations where the officers lost their lives, and became hubs of memorial flowers and remembrances. Each cross had the beehive-shaped shield of the Utah Highway Patrol, the name of the fallen state trooper, the year of death, and their badge number. However, atheists filed a lawsuit, the courts decided the crosses violated the Establishment Clause, and the Utah memorial crosses were removed.

So why do I remind you about crosses being removed from public land in this cheerful book about Christmas? Isn't this about the birth of Jesus, not His crucifixion? Well, ten-second sound bites in television interviews are a ridiculous, inefficient way to make a point—especially when you're being interviewed by buffoons on the air who won't let you complete your thought. So I'm writing about it here. The point is, as we know, the problem many people have with Christmas is found in the word's first syllable. The "war on Christmas" is actually part of a much larger battle to secularize our culture and get rid of any remnants of Christ.

But of course, Joe McScrooge isn't only irritated with crosses. He is also shocked at the courthouse Nativity scene.

THE MANGER

Roger Ailes, the president of Fox News Network, once asked me, "What the h-ll is so offensive about putting up a plastic Jewish family on my lawn at Christmastime?" And he's right. Nativity scenes are rather simple representations of Mary, Joseph, and the baby Jesus, composed of a wooden shack, some hay, a baby doll, and a string of Christmas lights. Other displays are elaborate, life-size tableaux, with hand-carved statues and real animals keeping watch through the night. Regardless of how elaborate they are, they've been at the epicenter of a contentious legal struggle for the past few years, one that reveals the legal and cultural battle surrounding the "war on Christmas."

Beautiful Santa Monica, California, was known for its elaborate Christmas displays and used to be nicknamed "the City of the Christmas story" because of its decades-long tradition of multi-stall displays set up in Palisades Park. Since 1953, churches put up these scenes, right next to the beach, for the public to enjoy. But in 2009, atheist Damon Vix set up a booth right next to the Nativity scenes with a sign. On one side, the sign had an alleged quote from Thomas Jefferson:

RELIGIONS ARE ALL ALIKE—FOUNDED

ON FABLES AND MYTHOLOGIES

On the other, the sign read:

HAPPY SOLSTICE

The following year, he put up the same display, right next to the Nativity scenes. Of course he was simply exercising his right of free speech, and while he may be trying to offend, none of us has a right to silence him. In 2011, however, he upped the ante.

He and other like-minded individuals decided to petition the government for permits for more and more displays. The permits were real requests, but the religions they supposedly represented were not quite kosher. For example, they requested a display honoring the "Pastafarian religion," which would include the "great Flying Spaghetti Monster." The city granted their permits. Out of twenty-one displays, eighteen were atheistic. Two Christmas displays had traditional Nativity scenes, the Jewish display showcased a menorah, and the atheist displays were designed to provoke and offend. One sign read:

SEASON OF THE WINTER SOLSTICE: LET REASON
PREVAIL. THERE ARE NO GODS, NO DEVILS,
NO ANGELS, NO HEAVEN OR HELL. THERE IS
ONLY OUR NATURAL WORLD. RELIGION IS BUT
A MYTH AND SUPERSTITION THAT HARDENS
HEARTS AND ENSLAVES MINDS.

Another display had four images: Poseidon, Jesus, Santa Claus, and Satan, along with the text:

THIRTY-SEVEN MILLION AMERICANS KNOW MYTHS
WHEN THEY SEE THEM. WHAT MYTHS DO YOU SEE?

The signs caused an uproar, and many were vandalized. After tiring of refereeing the religious war, the city ended its nearly sixty-year-long Christmas story Nativity tradition.

You'd be wrong if you thought these kinds of attacks occur only on the Left Coast, in the blue states. The ACLU assisted the Arkansas Society of Freethinkers (a community of agnostics, humanists, and atheists) in a lawsuit that resulted in a ruling that allowed the ASF to set up a four-sided display at the state capitol. One side of their display celebrated the winter solstice and the other three educated passersby about their "Freethinker" organization. You can see a pattern emerging. The atheists are trying to make Nativity scenes such a pain for cities to maintain that the public officials will simply remove all religious displays entirely. Federal district judge Susan Webber Wright ruled over the hearing, which she ended by wishing people to have a "happy holiday, or solstice, or whatever."

And in that "whatever," celebrators of Christmas are left wondering how much further they're going to be bullied away from society.

SCHOOLS

Of course, Joe McScrooge wasn't only irritated by the crosses and the Nativity scenes. He was also angered by his son's school Christmas program. Public schools are the front lines of the cultural and legal battle for both the soul of our nation and the way we celebrate December 25.

For example, last year, a student group of Western Piedmont Community College in North Carolina was getting ready for their annual Christmas tree sale fund-raiser. Instead of being happy that their students were trying to raise money for their Angel Tree initiative—a program that gives presents to under-privileged children—the school was more concerned that students hadn't been politically correct in their advertisements. When the BEST Society submitted the appropriate forms to promote the sale, the school changed their announcement. Suddenly, the BEST Society was selling "holiday trees" instead of the oh-so-exclusionary Christmas trees. Potential customers were irritated by the change and refused to buy the evergreens. However, the school's community relations director didn't waver, saying, "We cannot market your trees in association solely with a Christian event."

In Honolulu, the Moanalua High School orchestra was busily practicing for their annual charitable program to raise money for impoverished African children. For the past six years, they had put on a concert with volunteers from the New Hope Church and had raised more than $200,000. In 2012 they'd already sold six hundred tickets and were expecting to generate more than $30,000 in donations for their charity. But four days before the performance, the Hawaii Department of Education canceled the performance, bowing to pressure from a threatened lawsuit by the Hawaii Citizens for the Separation of State and Church.

Last November, Agape Church in Little Rock, Arkansas, invited the children of Terry Elementary School to attend an upcoming performance of *A Charlie Brown Christmas* at their church. Their program was based on the 1965 television special, which is one of my favorite things to watch at Christmas. I love the scene when the Peanuts gang sings "Hark, the Herald Angels Sing." I love it when Linus so lovingly wraps his blue blanket around Charlie Brown's scraggly tree. Mostly, I love the scene in which Linus recites the Scripture from the book of Luke, explaining to Charlie "what Christmas is all about." This two-minute segment of simple animation packs a punch more meaningful than all of the recent Christmas movies combined. The best part is when Linus gets to the words "Fear not," and then, as if realizing where his true security comes from, he drops his blanket. Perhaps the church in Little Rock wanted the kids from the elementary school to feel some of that same fearlessness, and that comforting Christmas spirit.

Pamela Smith, spokesperson for the Little Rock School District, told Fox News, "The teachers wanted to provide an opportunity for cultural enrichment for students through a holiday production and are supported by the principal. Because it will be held at a church, as some public events often are, a letter was sent home with students so parents who took exception and wished to have their children remain at school could do so."

No one complained to the school. However, one anonymous parent contacted the Arkansas Society of Freethinkers and began a campaign to get the event canceled. To its credit, the school board didn't cave in to the pressure. However, Pastor Happy Caldwell eventually announced the church wasn't going to go on with the program.

"Because of what this issue has become, as a church, it is not our desire to put hardworking, sacrificial teachers and cast members in harm's way."

In harm's way.

Think about that for a moment. A church was concerned that offering a popular production to elementary school students in a voluntary program would place school employees in legal jeopardy. See the power of an offended atheist?

Yet as the Scrooges flex their illegitimately gained legal muscles in red states and blue, all hope is not lost. To persevere—to "keep Christmas well"—our public officials need to be just a little bit savvy and just a little bit brave.

I'll tell you how.

Heather and our black lab, Woosha, at Hatcher
Pass in 1980. After Christmas, we'd take
advantage of the remaining Christmas break to
go ptarmigan hunting on our skis.

2

Knowing the End
from the Beginning

*There are no easy answers but there are simple
answers. We must have the courage to do what
we know is morally right.*

—RONALD REAGAN

"You're probably pushing it, Madam Mayor," my
favorite City Hall employee cautioned as I was
walking out the door there one December evening in
the late 1990s.

Our dear old finance director, Erling Nelson, had
served our city for years, and I'd known him even
longer. I'd even babysat his kids when I was a teenager. While I served two terms on the City Council,
we worked countless hours together poring over city
budgets. I always proposed slashing them, but he
liked me anyway. Erling was giving me both political

and friendly advice while waving me out the door that day.

"Come with me, then," I replied.

"Don't say I didn't warn you," he said with a chuckle and a friendly wave. I grinned, and continued through the door on my way to the city park's lawn.

When I arrived, our local service club was already busy setting up the annual Nativity scene, but they stopped long enough to do the usual hugs all around. Our Rotarians and yellow-vested Lions Club members faithfully and humbly tasked themselves with this Christmas tradition (plus so many other needed projects, like Spring Clean-Up Day) in Wasilla every year. I loved these guys. And gals. One Lion, who happened to be former mayor Harold Newcomb, walked me over to the bins full of hay, composite lambs, and an old, chipped, snow-weathered donkey. He was looking for the bin labeled BABY JESUS.

"I don't know how much longer we'll get to do this," he confided. "Cities are getting sued left and right for acknowledging the true meaning of Christmas nowadays. And the local politicians with the guts to stand up to the protests are caving in like an Alyeska avalanche."

I'd already heard the preemptive defense some of our Rotarians had prepared in case they needed to counter any criticism. It had become the hip thing that year across America to force anyone and everyone to abort Christ from Christmas. "Let me fight it for you, Mr. Newcomb," I said. "Tradition and truth are on our side. What's the worst that can happen? Some yahoo from outside Alaska gets wind of this and sues? Shoot, no one 'outside' has even heard of Wasilla. Let's do this, and be assured I have your back. I know you have mine." Just then, I got goose bumps. This may have been because I'd replaced my warm Bunny Boots for cool, high-heeled leather ones when I left City Hall. But more likely it was because I loved the idea of defending my hometown in a worthy cause. It was invigorating. "You tell your Lions we're good."

We found Jesus. Harold pulled out the storage bin, and I wiped the dust from his baby face.

"Is there anyone who'll cause trouble locally?" I asked. I trusted Mayor Newcomb. He was a lot like Erling. I'd grown up with his kids and played on the girls' softball team with his daughters for years. We used his hayfield as a makeshift ball field until developers bought it and built a Sears store on first base.

"Who'll cause trouble? *You*," he said with a wink. "As long as you let this display get put up every year."

"Wasilla has displayed this scene every year since . . ." I paused, racking my brain for this piece of information. I noticed the Mary figurine was stored below the sheep. That couldn't have been a fun way to spend a year. "Well, as long as I can remember."

"Times have changed."

"You're right," I said, standing Mary up and checking to make sure she survived the storage shed. Her pale blue scarf covered her hair, and her face was frozen in perpetual admiration for her child, Jesus. Now, that's not a bad way to be stuck, I thought. "Times have changed. But we haven't."

I knew I'd be criticized and challenged for sanctioning the Nativity scene all six years that I served as mayor. But I didn't care. I was thankful for the opportunity to declare traditional beliefs during the most joyous season of the year. I put the Nativity scene in the same category as the National Day of Prayer. When I was mayor, we hosted the event on the lawn at City Hall. When I was governor, we hosted it on the steps of our state capitol. I welcomed any protest, because it gave the perfect opportunity to strengthen our spines; if you can't handle protests, then it's hard to handle the other challenges of the job. As a free American aware of the value of our First Amendment rights, I know these are battles worth fighting.

I knew some people might find it controversial, but I joined in the Nativity event, Christmas after glorious

Christmas. I made it a family event. I would drag the kids out on snowy, freezing cold days to ceremonially put the baby Jesus doll in the Nativity scene, then head over to the city's pioneer town site to light the old schoolhouse and post office, then judge the gingerbread house decorations. That's how we kicked off the holiday season.

Actually, liberals should love the Wasilla Nativity scene. Why? Because the home of this plastic Jewish family is recycled. In a former life, it was an old hippie van. When the service clubs got hold of it, it was cut in half lengthwise, half removed, and covered with plastic to enclose a hay-filled manger scene. To this day, the city proudly displays the scene at the entrance to our town—right next to the three LED-lit moose and a multicolored Christmas tree—on the shores of Wasilla Lake.

Driving by the humble display last year with my sister, Molly, it occurred to me the torn Scooby-Doo van might not be the prettiest backdrop for the holy scene. "Well, look on the bright side," Molly pointed out. "It's never been vandalized."

"You're right," I told her. "Even if it were vandalized, we'd probably never notice."

For years, I've been concerned with protecting these public Christmas displays, even in my role in local government. Why would I get the kids up early and drag them out to the Nativity display every year? Believe me, they asked me the same question. When the kids were young they were too busy scarfing down oatmeal, looking for snow boots, and gamely slipping on gloves on the way to the ceremony to pause for a more in-depth discussion—but, Track, Bristol, Willow, and Piper, please pay attention now as I more fully explain why I prioritized that annual trek. (Trig came along, too, but he's usually game for the festivities and all things Christmas.)

I do hope you all teach your children these lessons, too, because a great deal is at stake.

Many of you may remember the late Christopher Hitchens, the atheist who famously wrote the 2007 best seller *God Is Not Great*—a manifesto for the irreligious. Not as many people realize he had a Christian brother, Peter, who later wrote a book called *Rage Against God*, which tells the moving story of his own journey to faith.

Peter had been a Moscow correspondent in the late 1980s, when the Soviet Union was breaking down. While there, he was able to witness a society in moral collapse, when churches were closed, priests and nuns were persecuted, and Christian education for kids was forbidden. He writes:

"I am also baffled and frustrated by the strange insistence of my anti-theist brother that the cruelty of Communist anti-theist regimes does not reflect badly on his case and on his cause. It unquestionably does . . . Soviet Communism is organically linked to atheism. . . . It used the same language, treasured the same hopes and appealed to the same constituency as atheism does today."

The logical result of atheism—a result we have seen right in front of our eyes, in one of the world's oldest and proudest nations—is severe moral decay. When anti-theism prevails, moral decay follows. In the Soviet Union that decay ultimately turned violent, as it did in Mao's China and Pol Pot's Cambodia. Atheism's track record makes the Spanish Inquisition seem like Disneyland by comparison.

Our Declaration of Independence states that we are endowed by our "Creator" with our rights, and it is astonishing that atheist critics think we will enhance our freedom by banishing that same Creator from the public square. Atheism's record would seem to dictate modesty, not aggression. Yet it is aggression that dominates activist atheism today.

Again and again, secular leftists complain that religion—especially Christianity—is a source of violence and repression, but in this country our

Judeo-Christian heritage is the source of the very free-doms they so angrily use to denounce Christ and to rid His very mention from the public square.

No matter how much the liberals protest, there's a relationship between Christianity and a healthy civilization, and we must resist their efforts to push God out of the culture, to characterize us as simple and superstitious, and to somehow say that religious education for children is even abusive.

We sing the national anthem before ball games to remind ourselves who we are and to literally pay tribute to the martial courage that birthed this nation.

We say the Pledge of Allegiance—yes, including the words "under God"—to declare that there are things that are more important than ourselves and to remind ourselves of the values that define our national character.

We put up Nativity scenes in tribute to the God who gave us life but also to acknowledge the very real history and identity of the vast majority of our citizens.

In each case, no one is required to participate, and people can vigorously disagree or even protest. Sit during the anthem, remain silent during the Pledge, or look away from the Nativity scene—each of those things is your right, and we not only respect your rights but defend them. But we also ask that you respect our decision to stand, our decision to speak, and our decision to declare our proud national heritage.

Symbols matter.

That Nativity scene in the old hippie van suddenly becomes a vital part of democracy.

Sound like a stretch?

Let's think this through. Without God as an objective standard, who's to say what's wrong and what's right? Morality becomes a matter of the human will, as each person decides what's right and what's wrong *for himself.* Since some of us are weak and some are strong, morality eventually becomes the will of the strong. This has been proven time and time again in history.

Peter Hitchens writes, "Why is there such a fury against religion now? Because religion is the one reliable force that stands in the way of the power of the strong over the weak. The one reliable force that forms the foundation of the concept of the rule of law."

As we watch the unfolding train wreck of Obamacare, as bureaucratic panels of supposed "experts" are making key decisions about your life and your death, as regulators are putting out tens of thousands of pages of rules that govern your doctors and your insurance companies, do you think their values matter? Do you think a bureaucrat or "expert" who honors God and values life and other inalienable rights will write rules that are different from a secular leftist who views babies as expendable and older Americans as crippling cost centers?

Leaders who value life as God-given, who zealously protect the inalienable, natural rights of men and women are far less likely to accumulate power, more likely to lay down the mantle of leadership willingly, and less convinced that they know what's best for all of us. There is only one perfect and perfectly wise man that ever lived.

He's the One in the Manger.

That modest manger leads to humility and respect for our fellow citizens. The empty public square leads to arrogance, and hatred, and contempt for those who disagree. Those who remove God from the cultural conversation are the same people who ask man to play God in public policy.

Had I canceled the Nativity, would there suddenly be a roving band of looters roaming the streets of Wasilla? Would anti-Christmas graffiti show up on buildings and bridges? Would churches be burned down? Of course not. But just as societies often start to collapse little by little, they are also preserved by small acts of respect. I was determined Wasilla would not contribute to our decline but would instead acknowledge the Source of all good things in our life and our nation. It was a small stand, but an important one.

And, thankfully, it's not even all that hard.

Encouragingly, there are many political leaders and ordinary citizens across this great country taking courageous stands.

Take Mayor Jim Fouts of Warren, Michigan. Every year, the city of Warren puts out a Christmas display that includes a Nativity scene, elves, and Santa's sleigh. But the Freedom from Religion Foundation saw one thing missing. They wanted him to include a sandwich-board sign that would read:

THERE ARE NO GODS, NO DEVILS, NO ANGELS,
NO HEAVEN OR HELL. THERE IS ONLY OUR
NATURAL WORLD. RELIGION IS BUT A MYTH
AND SUPERSTITION THAT HARDENS HEARTS
AND ENSLAVES MINDS. STATE/CHURCH
KEEP THEM SEPARATE.

Now, that really puts ya in the Christmas spirit, doesn't it? Note the similarity of this sign to the one I previously mentioned in Santa Monica. This shows these guys aren't just a few malcontents with lawyers who wreak havoc. They are a part of a larger, orchestrated attempt to strip our heritage from America. Mayor Fouts, however, refused to take down the Nativity scene *or* add the ridiculous sign.

"I felt that to allow them to put their sandwich board sign up was an offensive act against religion," he said. "And it wasn't exercising freedom of religion or freedom of speech. It was exercising the desecration and destruction of religion."

But here's my favorite part.

"I believe the Constitution deals with freedom of religion, and not freedom against religion or freedom to repress religion," he said. "I think it is a battle worth fighting."

The Sixth U.S. Circuit Court of Appeals agreed.

In *Freedom from Religion Foundation v. City of Warren*, Judge Jeffrey Sutton wrote that the U.S. Constitution "does not convert these displays into a seasonal public forum, requiring governments to add all comers to the mix and creating a poison pill for even the most secular displays in the process." That meant the mayor was well within his rights. Otherwise, "Veterans Day would lead to Pacifism Day, the Fourth of July to Non-Patriots Day, and so on."

Of course, people of all political stripes should be able to agree on this commonsense approach to holidays. But it took that one courageous mayor to draw a line in the sand—or the snow, since it was Michigan—and say, "No more."

Public officials trying to figure out the legality of their Nativity displays can learn a great deal from Mayor Fouts. Here are a couple more tips:

First, be patient. In the Santa Monica public forum from the previous chapter, the city shut down everyone's free speech simply to avoid controversy. Had the city merely been more patient, the atheists would likely have tired of their malicious campaign, and Christmas—which has lasted for so many centuries—would have endured. Why? Because faith endures longer than mockery.

Second, if you do have public displays on city property, use both secular and religious imagery in the display and you'll almost certainly be okay. If you want to have a Nativity scene, place it in the context of various holiday items like Mayor Fouts did—for example, also include jingle bells, a Christmas tree, a menorah, or the jolly chubby old man himself, St. Nick. The courts tend not to like Nativity scenes isolated from other holiday imagery. However, the case is much better if they exist in the context of multiple other displays.

Chances are, you aren't the local mayor or state governor; you're more likely a hardworking American without ties to government titles. (If so, count your blessings.) Does that mean you're home free?

Not really. Seventy-six-year-old John Satawa's family had been setting up a Nativity scene for more than sixty years on a public median between Mound and Chicago Roads in—once again—Warren, Michigan. Though they'd never received a complaint against the manger scene during those six decades, the Freedom from Religion Foundation filed a complaint in 2008 saying the display—you guessed it—was illegal. The Macomb County Road Commission caved, asking Satawa to remove his Nativity scene within thirty days for lack of a permit.

Many people would have wrung their hands, taken down the display, and grumbled while resenting the fact that America had become such a religiously hostile place. But not Satawa. First, he played by their rules. He submitted a permit request, along with photos of the proposed display, dimensions, and a description. Very soon, though, he learned that his permit had been denied because it contained religious content.

That's when he contacted a lawyer—who also happened to be a marine—who fought back. It took four years. And, having battled my share of ridiculous lawsuits, I know those four years weren't easy. Or inexpensive.

But the Satawa family prevailed in the courts, and the sixty-year tradition was able to continue.

"We filed this lawsuit in 2009 and it's not until 2012 that we got our results," said attorney Robert Muise. "You know, Ronald Reagan famously stated that our rights aren't handed down to us through the bloodstream, they constantly have to be fought for and protected. They could become extinct in one generation and we're seeing our rights, especially our right to free exercise of religion and our right to freedom of speech, being abridged and we have to stand up and fight."

Hoohah! I couldn't have said it better myself.

The moral of the story is simple: Fight. Fight smart, but fight. It's astounding how many times the ACLU or the FFRF and their allies win without even having to fight the battle. Risk-averse cities cave or frustrated citizens throw up their hands and move on.

Yet this is the wrong response, because it empowers atheist activists and enables them to exploit their national influence.

If your city or your school board gets an ACLU letter, don't panic. (The idea is not far-fetched; a few years ago the ACLU sent Christmas warning letters to virtually every school board in Tennessee.) There are actually thousands of conservative lawyers who are trained in the First Amendment eager to help; some organizations will help for free. They'll evaluate the situation, recommend changes that might be needed, and then fight for you if the case is solid. Three decades ago the ACLU was essentially unchallenged, but it now has formidable opposition.

If a town tells you that you can't put up your own display, don't take that as the last word. Even well-meaning town officials make mistakes all the time—intimidated by the mere thought of a lawsuit. Anytime someone tells you that you can't speak, whether it's about Christmas or anything else, get a second opinion.

Don't give up easily. It may seem that political correctness dictates your surrender, because swimming upstream takes such effort and resources. As I've said before, only dead fish go with the flow.

Be tenacious.

But be smart.

A person I know once said, "Stupid for Jesus is still stupid." While the ACLU overreaches all the time, sometimes (and this is sad to say) the law is on their side. Rather than beat your head against the brick wall of a federal court, that's when you pull back, rethink, and creatively explore new forms of expression. Does the Christmas display need a Christmas tree? Add the tree. Does it need Rudolph? Add Rudolph. Kids will be delighted, the manger is more likely to stay, and—best of all—you'll trigger a conversation about Christmas that will explore its meaning to the secular and religious alike.

Finally, don't despair. Through it all, the God who created the heavens and the earth is sovereign. As the Psalmist said, "Why do the nations rage and the peoples plot in vain?" No scheme of an atheist or secular activist can defeat God's plans and purposes. Our nation is in His hands. The battle between good and evil is as old as mankind, and though the other side may win a round, the sun will rise tomorrow, we'll stiffen our spines, and we'll fight again. But we don't fight with desperation or resentment. Rather, we fight with the confidence of people who know the manger was just the beginning. We fight with the boldness that comes with knowing how the story ends.

Here's a hint: It ends well.

In our home, athletics have always been
a priority . . . and we didn't stop for
Christmas vacation. Here I am in a pre-
Christmas "Fun Run" in the snow in 1981.

3

The Real Thing

For it is good to be children sometimes, and
never better than at Christmas, when its
mighty Founder was a child Himself.

—CHARLES DICKENS, *A CHRISTMAS CAROL*

The early-morning sky was full of stars on Christmas in 1981. We walked out onto the porch, looked up, and saw a short but breathtaking wave of the aurora borealis. I pulled my arms around my chest and breathed it all in. You couldn't create a more perfect backdrop.

"Wow," Heather said, almost to herself as she looked at the purple, pink, green, and aqua northern lights. A perfect welcome-home gift. My older siblings had been at college, and I was so excited to have the whole family at home again during their break. "I sure have missed the 'dancing hem of heaven,'" she said, using a common description of the northern lights.

"They don't have this in Kirkland," I teased. She was attending college in Washington State, and I liked to joke about how far south she now lived.

Our breath hung heavily in the air, and eventually we could no longer stand the cold. Not that we wanted to delay the long-anticipated gift-opening ritual. On Christmas morning, Dad had two rules. First, he made sure the kids served Mom a cup of hot coffee before the first bow was ripped off. Second, and more difficult to obey, was that we had to open presents one person at a time. This was an ironclad rule no one violated, no matter how impatient they grew as the previous gift-opener took care (and precious time) to preserve the packaging while opening a treasured present.

But no one ever had to wait for me. I was always eager to open the presents while Mom encouraged us, "Now, save that bow for next year." (This habit became so ingrained that I still save the nicer bows.)

Every Christmas, we devoured a huge homemade cinnamon roll wreath dotted with red and green cherries made by our friend Kris Carter. Before we even finished licking the icing off our fingers, Mom called Kris to thank her.

"You always add joy to our holiday mornings," she said.

Oh so slowly Alaska's dawn drew nearer midday, but it was so dark outside we couldn't tell. Inside our little house on Lucille Street, we still had presents to open. That was our main focus. One by one, the number of presents diminished, and my anticipation grew. My younger sister, Molly, dug under the tree and handed me an eight-by-twelve-inch box.

"That's it," she said, with a finality that indicated I was down to my last present.

I always tried to judge the gift from its box, which is harder to do than you might think. Frequently, I'd wait to open the last, perfectly wrapped present only to find practical but not very exciting wool socks. This one, however, felt substantial—it had to be electronic. I breathed a sigh of relief.

Unless Mom had wrapped up the 1981 season's gimmicky Pet Rock, I may have actually saved the best gift for last. It was pretty heavy—definitely too heavy for socks, at least. I removed the huge blue bow, put it in Mom's "save for next year" bag, and pressed the sparkly snowflake-covered box against my ear. I gave it a gentle shake.

"Ha. I can't hear anything," I whispered to Molly, who was busy checking out the last packages beneath the dry needles and strands of fallen tinsel. The spruce had been vibrant and beautiful for the month it stood in our home, but it had finally dried out. I noticed it still spread that unmistakable Christmas aroma throughout our house.

"What did you expect it to do?" she laughed. "Start playing a song?"

Molly was amused by my anticipation, but I didn't think it was funny. I was the only girl on the Warriors basketball team without a newfangled yellow mini-tape recorder. The Sony Walkman had revolutionized the way people listened to music, and I'd been left twiddling my thumbs while my friends bobbed their feathered-banged heads to "Jessie's Girl" and "9 to 5" on their headphones (I was more of a Van Halen and Joan Jett type girl, and to get into a game-day mind-set I'd listen to *Back in Black*). Because of the sparse population and vastness of our state, our teams often traveled hundreds of miles to get to the next town to play another team. Traveling to play the mighty Valdez Buccaneers forced our volunteer bus driver, former state trooper Dave Churchill, to haul us on roads through twenty-feet-deep snow over Thompson Pass. Today this area is the site of many ESPN X-Games and extreme sports competitions; back then it was just a treacherous but amazing ride. As we rode along, wrapped tight in down sleeping bags nestled on cold, crackly vinyl seats, the miles passed beyond the frosted windshield of our old school bus. I sat there dreaming of listening to my own cassettes instead of the tire chains clanking beneath me.

On the weekends, I babysat and had janitorial duties at the office building that housed Dollarhide, DeCamp, and Brown (Wasilla's local surveyors and architect firm), but I dutifully set aside all of my paychecks for college. A Sony Walkman cost ninety-nine dollars, which was about ninety-nine more than I had for such an extravagance. There was no way I could have afforded to buy one myself.

Just as I was about to tear into my final present to reveal my new Walkman, the dogs started barking. "Hey, kids," Dad said, "Rufus and Woosha are hungry. Go feed them before we open the last ones."

With great force of will, I put down my present and took a deep breath. I'd waited this long to have my own music, I thought, what's another few minutes?

My brother, Chuck, hustled our German shepherd out the door and kicked and finally pried loose the frozen bowl belonging to our black lab. Even though we'd given her water just a few hours before outside on the porch, the tin bowl was as solid as a rock. I tried not to think of this inconvenience. In just a few moments, I'd be the proud owner of my very own Walkman. No more community "867-5309" on repeat, blaring from my teammates' boom boxes. On the next road trip, I'd listen to my own songs. Heart's "Barracuda," here I come!

Finally, I sat back down and picked up the gift again.

"Someone stoke the woodstove," Dad said. When I looked up in disbelief, he smiled. We girls were toasty warm in our matching handmade long flannel night-gowns, which our Grandma Helen Sheeran sewed for us every year. He knew he was driving me crazy.

"Come on, Dad," I protested. "The fire's still roar-ing! Let me open this, please, and I'll stack a whole cord of wood later," I bargained.

He smiled and motioned for Molly and me to go on and open our last two presents. I couldn't stand it when my sister began opening hers first.

Seriously?

I knew I was supposed to wait my turn, but it took her forever to open her gift, then ooh and aah over how awesome she was going to look, thanks to her very own curling iron.

Finally, I slid my finger under the tape of my very last present. Everyone was watching. Molly was gig-gling. I figured it was silly sisterly jealousy, because I was about to get the coolest gift ever.

I reminded myself, for my parents' sake, to feign surprise. Shoot, they'd gone to all the trouble of traveling to Anchorage to buy the one and only thing I wanted, no doubt a sacrifice on a schoolteacher's salary (though I considered it a matter of social life and death). At least I could pretend I didn't see it coming. One last glance up and one more "Ha" mouthed at Molly and I pulled off the wrapping paper.

Act surprised, Sarah.

But there was no need to act.

My jaw dropped. It was yellow, all right. But it was a brand-new *Webster's Dictionary*!

Molly cracked up. Dad's grin wrapped around his face. Mom smiled and said, "I love you." Molly laughed even harder.

There would be no singing into the hairbrush and dancing around our shared bedroom anytime soon. But over the years, that unexpected Christmas present has turned into one of my family's most treasured stories. We laugh about how it so perfectly describes what it was like to grow up in the Heath residence. As disappointed as I was for that fleeting moment that winter day (or a bit longer, especially on those cold journeys to away games), I knew my good parents were teaching me a lesson I would remember forever.

Words matter.

When people hear of the "war on Christmas," they sometimes don't get it. Americans live in the red-and-green mistletoed world of Christmas in December, hearing "Santa Baby" on a perpetual loop at the mall, hushing the kids in the Swagger Wagon when "Grandma Got Run Over by a Reindeer" comes on the radio, and dealing with Christmas ads even before November's Thanksgiving turkey has time to cook to the appropriate internal temperature. If there is a "war on Christmas," they must wonder, surely the green glitter and constant car-with-a-gigantic-bow ads mean Christmas is winning the battle.

Sure, the commercial aspects of Christmas are stronger than ever, but the essence of Christmas is being lost in the shuffle. And that's at least partly by design. What is the essence of Christmas? The magic of Christmas morning and seeing the joy that comes when your kids discover Santa really did give the new Lego sets—or dictionaries—they desperately wanted?

Actually, giving gifts to children (and family, and friends) is wonderful, fun, and so appropriate. In very large families like we have on both the Palin and Heath sides, we each draw names now out of a hat at Thanksgiving and prepare for one main gift to give to the one name we've drawn. Otherwise we'd grow debt as fast as Nancy Pelosi. And we all promise this year we'll stick to the rules and give only *one* gift. But invariably we break the rule. Don't we all eventually realize Mom was right when she said it really *is* better to give than to receive? Either that, or the older we get, the more we turn into Mom. My mom, Sally, always insists she neither wants nor needs anything material for Christmas or birthdays.

"Save your money, honey. Just make me a homemade card," Sally suggests. "Or write me a poem."

I must be turning into Sally. Because about five years ago, I made the same suggestion to Piper, who compiled beautiful prose about her love for her mama. I wanted nothing else.

"You are good at work," she crayoned. "I make you laff," she added. "You are pretty as a plant," she concluded.

It's my favorite and will hang in the kitchen hallway forever.

Yes, buying presents can be great fun, but it can teach us things about God, too. Last Christmas morning my son Track was home from a deployment in Afghanistan and he got to videotape his nephew, Tripp, reacting to Santa's visit the night before.

"Wow. All this for *me*?" Tripp squeals as the video captures his bright wide eyes and upraised arms. "And I wasn't even very good!"

"That's cool," Track said, smiling. This may have been Tripp's first lesson in unearned, amazing grace.

Gift giving is great fun, but also pretty superfluous to the actual meaning of the holiday. Christmas is, of course, based on a historical event: the birth of Jesus. Virtually everyone—from your kids' schoolteachers, to the bartenders at the Salty Dog Saloon, to the self-proclaimed academic elites at modern universities—agree that Jesus actually lived. While people may passionately disagree about His importance, there's no legitimate disagreement over the fact He was born.

We aren't really sure when exactly. In the fourth century AD, the Catholic Church decided to celebrate Christmas on December 25, even though the Bible isn't very specific about the timing. Most believe they chose this time of the year to coordinate the Christmas festivities with the already existing ancient pagan festivals—for example, the Roman Saturnalia and the winter solstice traditions. But over time those old pagan celebrations faded into obscurity because they weren't grounded in much of anything but myth, while Christmas gained ever more prominence and meaning.

(Does that mean Christians won the "war on Saturnalia"? You bet. And it shows the incredible power of even new traditions to shape culture.)

Whatever the precise roots of the holiday, we now know that when Pope Julius I declared the official date of Christmas—"the Feast of the Nativity"—the faithful had another significant holy day.

So fast-forward a few years and jump over to a different continent. "Christmas" became an American federal holiday in 1870, when President Ulysses S. Grant signed a bill the House and Senate had already overwhelmingly passed. In this country, our federal holiday does not honor the agricultural gods of Rome or the pagan rituals of the winter solstice. Here in America, Christmas marks Christ's birth, a moment of unquestioned historical, cultural, and religious significance. (This is revealed in the actual name of the holiday: *Christ*mas.)

During Christmas, people aren't forced to worship Jesus, buy presents, or put up a tree. They still get to enjoy all the liberties that make this country unique and magnificent. If so inclined, people have the right to sit in a circle in the forest and hum songs of gratitude to Mother Earth while taking turns hugging bark on December 25. But it doesn't change the underlying reason for the federal holiday. That's why, traditionally, it has been celebrated with songs like "O Little Town of Bethlehem," "Away in a Manger," "Hark! The Herald Angels Sing," and—of course—Handel's *Messiah*. Christmas is based on the story of a census, a young mom-to-be, NO VACANCY signs at the Bethlehem Motel 6, and that very humble manger.

You almost wouldn't know it these days. In our commercial world, we often don't have "Christmas" anymore, just a season called the "holidays." Which holidays? Let's see, there's Hanukkah, Kwanzaa, New Year's, and what else? Never mind, let's just buy more gifts to celebrate whatever days are important to you. It's the gifts that are important, right?

But if presents are the entire point, which it seems like they have become, store marketers will start to change their language to be as "inclusive" as possible. We wouldn't want the few remaining Saturnalia celebrators to deprive their kids of good solstice treats, eh? The more sales the better!

Take Target, for example. In 2005, shoppers noticed there was something a little off about their shopping experience under the big red bull's-eye. Though the signs in the stores were printed in the traditional Christmas colors, the language didn't include the actual, official name of the holiday. Some said, SAVINGS OF THE SEASON while others said GATHER ROUND.

The stockings were hung by the register with care— for sale—under the shelf tag TRADITIONAL HOLIDAY

STOCKINGS and Christmas ornaments were labeled TRADITIONAL HOLIDAY ORNAMENTS.

Christmas trees were labeled as merely FIR and PINE.

Their website had no mention of Christmas, either, instead including language like "Holiday Recipes" and "All Things Holiday." Even their shipping guidelines went to painfully great lengths to obscure the name of the holiday. "Get It by the 25th," it read. Of course, there are several holidays going on in December, but only one happened on that specific date. Why the ambiguity?

And it's not just Target. The classic movie *Miracle on 34th Street* forever etched a famous department store into our collective Christmas memories. Many visitors to New York stroll by Macy's to see its elaborate window displays or drop in to buy something from the iconic destination. However, in 2004, even Macy's signs suddenly became holiday nonspecific, too.

In 2005, Lowe's proudly sold "holiday trees," at least according to the large signs that hung across their stores all across America.

In 2011, Walgreens' twenty-four-page nationwide circular used the word *holiday* thirty-six times without one mention of Christmas.

One of the most egregious examples of Christmas heavy-handedness comes from—believe it or not—Wal-Mart. Now, Wal-Mart is huge in my home-town. They have all kinds of records at this local store, like selling more miles of duct tape in the Wasilla store than anywhere else. I kid you not. The 2003 award is on the wall. The Wasilla store sold 325 miles of duct tape, which—the company calculated—meant they sold 314 feet of duct tape to each Wasilla resident.

As mayor of the city I was asked to conduct a wedding of two sweet young Wal-Mart associates inside the store, down a nicely decorated aisle. It was my pleasure.

Wal-Mart is big in our little town. An intrigued, or bored, reporter once asked me why I thought that was so. I responded by stating the obvious.

"Because it's cheap," I said. "People want a good deal."

She seemed perplexed, like the box-store-type experience was quite foreign to her. I let her continue and tried not to laugh.

"But in Wasilla, Wal-Mart isn't just a store," her astute journalism skills led her to declare; "it's an event."

"Okay," I said before finishing the interview. "But it's a cheap event."

But not everyone has the privilege of living near Wasilla's Wal-Mart. So the retail giant's website features a search engine to find products more easily for online purchases. But Catholic League president Bill Donohue noticed something odd about Wal-Mart's search engine one Christmas. He learned that entering the word "Hanukkah" would bring a potential customer to a page detailing more than two hundred Hanukkah-related items. If a customer entered the word "Kwanzaa," he was taken to a page that detailed seventy-seven products related to the African heritage celebration. However, if a customer typed in "Christmas," the customer was taken to a landing page that read, "We've brought you to our 'Holiday' page based on your search." There was a second link that would take a customer to a Christmas products page, but it's interesting that only the term "Christmas"—not the names of other holidays—brought up the generic page. Why were Kwanzaa and Hanukkah perfectly fine to mention by name, but not Christmas? Additionally, Wal-Mart began encouraging its employees to wish customers "Happy Holidays" instead of "Merry Christmas."

I could catalog dozens of examples of stores eliminating "Christmas" from their vocabulary. Is this *really* the biggest deal in the world? I can already hear the snickering from the pundits. A *New York Times* columnist wrote an article about the "war on Christmas" under the headline "My Favorite War," insinuating it's not really a big deal. After all, no one really dies in this "war." Yes, liberals love to deride this topic, invariably concluding with a sneer that words don't matter. They say we should be thankful for the spirit behind them and leave it at that. What does it matter that stores are using "Happy Holidays"? Obviously not everyone in America is an observant Christian, so isn't it simply easier to call it a "holiday" and move on? Isn't it just a sign in a store or a greeting from a cashier who's probably just waiting for his shift to end so he can beat feet out of there?

But the pundits are using their condescension to cover an obvious double standard.

Remember in chapter 1, when we talked about what a big deal it is to be religiously offended? Atheists and secular liberals have bent over backward to cater to the "offended observer." As you've already read, there have been multiple lawsuits filed—and won—by liberal lawyers representing "offended observers" at no cost to them, but at great cost to the accused and to taxpayers picking up the court fees.

So let me get this straight. If you're an offended atheist, you should make it a federal case, because hearing a word you don't want to hear is a big frickin' deal. Words are powerful. However, if you're an offended Christian, suddenly the power of language evaporates.

Words don't matter, they say. You're just overly sensitive when "Christmas" is relentlessly cleansed from our public vocabulary, and you should simply get over the fact that it has been replaced by something else.

Got it?

Me neither.

What the condescending Lamestream Media tries to do is this: They want the world to believe that an atheist customer who's outraged over a "Merry Christmas" greeting at the store is a hero, whose feelings are more important than a Christian customer who gets ticked over a "Happy Holidays" greeting. We're characterized instead as knuckle-dragging, bitter-clinging idiots.

But, unfortunately for all the liberals out there, we knuckle-draggers recognize a double standard when we see one. And we're fighting back.

In 2011, when the American Family Association alerted its members that Walgreens' circular never mentioned the word "Christmas," they were encouraged to shop elsewhere.

Walgreens immediately issued a response. "As Christmas Day draws closer, you'll see more references to the word 'Christmas.' That includes the message, 'Merry Christmas,' which will be on the front of our newspaper sales insert on December 25. We fully agree with you that—while we're helping customers celebrate a variety of holidays during this time of year—we should continue and increase the use of the word 'Christmas' when referring to items specifically for the Christmas holiday."

Lowe's customers similarly didn't appreciate the gigantic banners advertising HOLIDAY TREES.

Was there any other holiday except Christmas that used trees in their celebration? Was the company hoping to sell a fir to an Arbor Day enthusiast with a bad sense of timing? After hundreds of customers complained, Lowe's took the banners down and found the courage to mention the word "Christmas."

Target customers also pushed back against the corporation's non-Christmas "holiday" marketing scheme. After more than half a million customers signed an online pledge to boycott the chain, the store started to mention Christmas in their sales materials. Macy's executive vice president, Louis M. Meunier, responded to complaints from the "Committee to Save Merry Christmas" by promising to "work on expanding the efforts we began this year with regard to the use of the term 'Merry Christmas' in our signage."

What amazing examples of calm, cool, and collected concerned citizens using their free-speech rights to protest something that seems blatantly unfair. However, sometimes complaints weren't met with such receptivity. When a Wal-Mart customer complained to customer service about the new "Happy Holidays" greeting, she got a rather unusual—but telling—response. An employee named Kirby wrote back this snarky letter:

> Walmart is a world wide organization and must remain conscious of this. The majority of the world still has different practices other than "christmas" which is an ancient tradition that has its roots in Siberian shamanism. The colors associated with "christmas" red and white are actually a representation of the aminita mascera mushroom. Santa is also borrowed from the Caucuses, mistletoe from the Celts, yule log from the Goths, the time from the Visigoth and the tree from the worship of Baal. It is a wide wide world.

WTH, Kirby?

After news organizations published this ridiculous e-mail, a Wal-Mart spokesman apologized:

> We at Wal-Mart believe this e-mail between a temporary associate and one of our valued customers was entirely inappropriate. Its contents in no way represent the policies, practices or views

of our company. This associate, who was hired less than three weeks ago, is no longer employed by our company. Wal-Mart is proud to welcome customers of all faiths, and celebrants of all holidays. We sincerely apologize to any person or organization that was offended by the inappropriate and inflammatory comments made by this former associate.

Eventually, they even backed off from their generic "Happy Holidays" marketing strategy, too. "This year, we're not afraid to say, 'Merry Christmas,'" a Wal-Mart spokeswoman said in 2006.

Why on earth would retail giants go to such lengths to rid Christmas of its actual name? It reminds me of NBC's liberal medical editor, who was being interviewed on the *Today* show about Christmas anxiety. The problem with Christmas, she concluded, is not the high expectations or the rampant commercialization. "I don't like the religion part," she said. "I think religion is what mucks the whole thing up." After the other guests laughed in shock, she said, "That's what makes the holiday so stressful. I want the green tree, which smells good, and everyone's happy."

Can you imagine the uproar if an NBC guest had said, "Islam really screws up Ramadan. We should be concentrating on weight loss during our daily fasts, not Allah Akbar."

It just wouldn't ever happen, because NBC would invite on a guest *who actually practices the religion* and would ensure the guest demonstrated at least a modicum of sense and respect.

Sadly, stores and pundits aren't the only culprits making the word "Christmas" disappear. If you have kids at public school, as I do, chances are their two weeks off are now called WINTER BREAK on the sign outside the school. If you watch television during the end of the year, you'll hear a great deal about the fa-la-la-la-la-lidays, but very little about "Christmas."

Perhaps people find the word "Christmas" uncomfortable because it forces people to deal with the historical figure of Christ. Was He telling the truth when He claimed to be God's son? Why was He revered, then criticized and mocked, then crucified? If He really lived—and history proves He did—what did He mean to the world?

Now, I don't think corporate CEOs are avoiding the word "Christmas" to spare their customers or viewers any spiritual angst associated with being confronted by the name of the Savior. The good folks at Lowe's corporate headquarters weren't sitting around saying, "We want customers to be thinking of how to improve their deck, not how to improve their souls." Instead, the corporate honchos probably figured the all-encompassing "Happy Holidays" would offend the fewest number of customers.

Of course, Lowe's doesn't want to participate in the religious practices of their customers. They simply want to sell the most products to harried shoppers looking for last-minute gifts. Christmas sales are good and vital to the health of these retailers, and the prosperity of their employees. I don't resent good marketing.

But the store gets it wrong with this generic response. Dave Barry pointed out the lunacy of the bland terms when he wrote, "These days, people say 'Season's Greetings,' which, when you think about it, means nothing. It's like walking up to somebody and saying 'Appropriate Remark in a loud, cheerful voice.' But 'Season's Greetings' is safer, because it does not refer to any actual religion. Someday, I imagine, even 'Season's Greetings' will be considered too religious, and we'll celebrate the Holiday Season by saying 'Have a nice day.'"

I think what he's trying to say is that the "all things to all people" philosophy isn't as all-encompassing or neutral as these stores believe.

As my parents taught me, words matter. Here's an example:

A group of teenagers from the local mosque excitedly hangs a big, cumbersome banner announcing the upcoming Ramadan season. It's a hot June day, so they take a break for a bit and drink some Kool-Aid before finishing their project.

Well-meaning neighbors stroll by, see the banner, and wave. The teenagers are surprised when these neighbors return an hour later. One of the neighbors is carrying a rolled-up sign under his arm.

"Excuse us," he says. "We're fine with you celebrating Ramadan in whatever way you choose, but we made a different, more pleasant sign for you to use in public."

"Why?" questions one of the teens.

"Well, no one really knows what that Arabic writing means," he says.

"Ramadan Mubarak," the teenage girl explains, "means 'congratulations, it's Ramadan.' This is an exciting time of year for us."

"Uh-huh, right . . . but that makes some people feel . . ."

The guy's wife pipes in. " . . . uncomfortable."

"Yes," the man laughs. "Religion just gets people riled up, you know. It's so divisive. We're Lutheran, for example, but we generally keep that to ourselves, don'tcha know."

The teenagers watch as the man unrolls his alternative banner. It is blue, with a crescent moon in a summer sky. However, the banner doesn't mention Ramadan at all.

"You expect us to replace our banner with one that just says, 'Enjoy the summer holidays?'" the incredulous teenager asks. "We're not celebrating the Fourth of July here."

"Yes, but we wouldn't want to offend non-Muslim patriots, now, would we?"

Or consider another scene:

It's my birthday, and I can hardly wait to get out of the hotel for a big fat piece of cake. I'm on the road for a few days of speaking engagements and on this day find myself in Vegas. It's the week before Todd's two-thousand-mile snowmachine race across Alaska, so I'm thankful he could take time out of a rigorous Iron Dog training schedule to meet up with me to celebrate. I get dressed up, tease my hair as big as it will go (believing the old southern adage that "the higher the hair, the closer to heaven"), and run down to the lobby, where Todd is waiting to kick off my birthday weekend. I'm hoping we'll head to Michael's at

Southpoint, my favorite. Todd kisses me and smiles.

"Happy mid-February Day."

"Huh? What do you mean?" I ask.

"Well, a lot has happened on this day in history. How can I narrow down to just one event that might be more interesting to me than the next? Today is the day General Eisenhower was chosen to command the Allied armies in Europe, Bill Parcells was named head coach of the New York Jets, and Janet Reno was chosen to be the first female attorney general. This is a big darn day."

"Yes," I say, rolling my eyes, "but it's also my birthday."

"Do you not respect the Greatest Generation?" he responds, indignant. "General Eisenhower helped win World War II. Not to mention that Valentine's Day is coming up and Presidents' Day. And don't forget Groundhog Day."

I look at him, dumbfounded. "You're taking me for carrot cake in part to honor Janet Reno?"

"Listen, I think it's better to play it safe, and it's much more tolerant to just generally acknowledge there are many cool things going on this month. You're sounding a bit intolerant and uneducated, babe. Would you like to talk about it?"

So if the above scenario actually happened, how would I feel?

First, I'd be single before hooking up with this fictitious version of Todd.

Second, Todd's refusal to acknowledge the specific reason for our celebration would not make for a fun evening.

Similarly, the teenagers from the mosque would never stand for their Ramadan banner being replaced by a generic alternative. And they shouldn't.

When large stores make the decision to de-Christ Christmas—the fulcrum of the so-called holiday season—they might believe they're acting in the least offensive way. However, they're actually offending the millions of Americans who are celebrating for a very specific reason. While there are obviously other important holidays happening in December, it's odd and rude to lump them all into one category or to pretend the throngs of customers pouring through the doors are only looking for solstice gifts.

The stores know why the shoppers are there, because they depend on this Christian holiday to improve their bottom lines. No other holiday packs such a global economic punch. In December, the travel industry picks up as people go home to see their loved ones. Greeting card sales go through the roof. Bizarre crazes cause riots in the aisles for things like Cabbage Patch Dolls, Tickle Me Elmos, and the newest, funkiest Air Jordans . . . and those old Walkmans, too! People buy flowers and home decorations as they "deck the halls." Yes, the Christmas tradition of gift giving brings in the dough. The day after Thanksgiving is called "Black Friday" because it's frequently the first time the stores are no longer "in the red" for the entire year. Christmas helps to employ millions of people and props up our entire retail economy.

This means the stores aren't surprised by all the faith-filled shoppers who walk through their doors to spend their hard-earned money. They relish it, they prepare for it, and they profit off it. This makes their insistence on secularizing the whole experience—by refusing to acknowledge why we're there—particularly offensive.

But not all places fumble the Christmas season. Bristol works at a dermatology office in Anchorage. Her boss, Dr. Cusack, displays a huge Nativity scene in the lobby, and the gals in the office say he leaves it up until the end of March. And the entire C Street section of Anchorage lights up when Kriner's Diner proclaims its Christmas spirit. (They even printed a little note on the little diner's menu: " . . . and we still say Merry Christmas.") In Wasilla, we, of course, have our retro-hippie bus manger scene on city property and even an ecumenical church service on Christmas morning held inside our public hockey rink. About a mile away the longtime family-owned Brown's Electric marquee spells out:

JESUS IS THE REASON FOR THE SEASON

And small-business owners farther south celebrate the season well, too. For example, in Kennewick, Washington, the owner of Jesse's Lawn Maintenance proudly showed us his Nativity scene. Right there on the front lawn of his business stood the "Three Wise Men Still Seeking Him," along with Mary, Joseph, the babe, and the herd. He told us he put this up every year, has never heard any complaints, and receives tons of cards and thank-yous. In Richland, Washington, my uncle Tom Johnson publicly showcases Christmas spirit at the Windermere Group One office. The real estate firm always decorates a Christmas tree, puts a sign outside wishing everybody a Merry Christmas, and uses lots of Christmas lights.

One of my favorite stores really goes the extra Bethlehem mile. In 1997, the popular craft store Hobby Lobby placed full-page Easter ads in the same newspapers in which their promotions regularly appear. The next year, they did it again, but bought full-page ads for Christmas as well. In 2007, they even went beyond their normal markets and advertised in the *New York Times* and the *Los Angeles Times*. Their ads—well done and attractive—have powerful messages. Last year's ad featured a silhouette of the three wise men heading to the manger, under the words "What Are You Seeking?" A previous year's ad simply stated Isaiah 9:6: "For to us a child is born . . . And he will be called Wonderful Counselor, Mighty God, Everlasting Father, Prince of Peace." Imagine that . . . They celebrate Christmas by mentioning Christ. Kudos to Hobby Lobby president Steve Green for running such a great company. In fact, recently I had the chance to meet this very attractive family (including his gorgeous daughters) at a conference in Washington, D.C. They seem to be on this business mission together, as a family. And my family loves their family business. Bristol decorated her house with Hobby Lobby items. Since we don't have a Hobby Lobby in Alaska, we took advantage of a road trip when Track and an Army buddy drove a truck and trailer from the Lower 48 up to Alaska. We stopped at Hobby Lobby first thing and loaded up the truck with "essentials" from one of our favorite stores, then sent the soldiers on their way.

When retail chains try their hardest to separate the "reason" from "the season," they're actually doing a disservice to people of all faiths.

Isn't the desire for a Christ-less Christmas not all that different from the secular Left's desire for a Christ-less, well, everything? The Left wants to see our faith-filled population do good deeds, serve the poor, be kind to their neighbors, and give generously, without all that messy and "divisive" Jesus and religion talk. But if they actually paid more attention, studies show Christians are America's most generous givers. So what really would happen if that silly NBC commentator could snap her fingers and make "all that religion stuff" just go away? Without faith, I doubt we'd have the love in our hearts that compels one to give, to volunteer, to be kind and loving to our neighbors, and to aspire to live the Golden Rule.

Without faith, we'd be, well, the secular Left—a group that data shows to be notoriously stingy with their time, money, and pleasant attitudes, and that believes "compassion" is best represented by a failed welfare state that traps millions in lifelong poverty and despair.

No, thanks.

Many people know the "feel" of Christmas—the warm glow from the homes, the smiles from strangers, the carolers knocking at the door, the smell of chestnuts wafting through the streets (though I've never smelled nor even seen a chestnut roasting), and the general feeling of hope and goodwill toward our fellow man. Though it's not created on Madison Avenue, advertisers capture some of that spirit quite brilliantly.

Who can forget that iconic Coca-Cola commercial from the seventies? The song begins, "I'd like to buy the world a home and furnish it with love. Grow apple trees and honeybees and snow-white turtle doves." (Yep, it was the seventies.) Or that classic Norelco commercial that had Santa zip through the snowy hills on a "Noelco" razor. Or the simple but effective commercial by Hershey, featuring their yummy candy Kisses playing "Jingle Bells"? Or when Peter came home from college for Christmas, awakening his sleeping family with a hot pot of Folger's coffee? Or any of the Budweiser ads that feature those gorgeous Clydesdales. Bud taught us all to declare, "I love ya, man, I really do." And we felt okay saying it.

Advertisers are savvy enough to try to encapsulate that certain "spirit" of Christmas, which exists far above the actual gifts. Unlike our previous examples of companies shunning Christmas, these commercials tap into the joy of Christmas pretty effectively. But in a different way they are diluting the true meaning of

Christmas as well. The commercials are always at least slightly tainted by the underlying assumption that the product alone is what would really top off your holiday. Want to have a *really* merry Christmas? Drink Bud, sip Folger's, eat Hershey's (hard for me to argue that one), shave your face the way Santa would if he didn't have to maintain his long, snowy beard. But this misses the mark.

The thing is, gifts can't really bring ultimate joy. Parents, I don't have to tell you this. How many times have your kids opened a present, only to end up playing with the box the gift came in? Sometimes gifts even bring a tinge of disappointment. (Thanks, Mom and Dad, for the dictionary!) How often have we sacrificed to buy a loved one something, only to sense a slight look of disappointment flashing across his face? (They wanted the cheetah-print iPod, not zebra, or a different action hero from a newer blockbuster, or jeans that sit a little higher on the hips to camouflage the muffin-top.) I remember years ago my sisters and I pooled funds to buy my teenage brother seventy dollars' worth of cleaning supplies for his room at his Sigma Alpha Epsilon frat house. We thought it the bestest, cleverest, most practical gift ever for him. He opened the box of Spic and Span, toilet paper, and Clorox and looked at us like we were from Mars (or the Heath residence).

Thankfully, there's that "religion stuff," which actually gives meaning to the season—and points us to the One who never fails, who gives truly "good gifts" to His children.

That catchy "I'd like to buy the world a Coke" jingle ended with "what the world wants today is the real thing." We all yearn for something real—for something beyond the torn wrapping paper crumpled on the floor on Christmas morning. No offense to Santa or Coca-Cola, but neither can ultimately satisfy the needs of our souls. When secular liberals and atheists try to rid society of the pesky effects of religion, they are unwittingly encouraging *more* commercialization of Christmas.

Christmas, the word and the holiday, is all based on an amazing historical event: God sent His son to earth. Immanuel. God with us. It's such a powerful story, it can lift our collective spirits in December regardless of how many fruitcakes have been regifted (or how many cans of Lysol and Pledge are wrapped in glittery bows; sorry, Chuck). The story elevates us regardless of how many "totally realistic" romantic diamond ads we've been unfortunate enough to watch, or how many garish ugly Christmas sweaters we've worn.

It's the real thing.

In 1986, the Heath kids were college
students, all at once! Me, Heather, Molly,
and Chuck—all home from college, reunited
and getting ready for our annual high school
alumni basketball games.

4

True Grit

How many kings come down from their thrones?

—DOWNHERE, IN THEIR SONG "HOW MANY KINGS"

I snuggled under the blanket on the couch in front of the television, awaiting my first viewing of *A Christmas Carol.* I was eager to enjoy a classic tale even though it was January. When I was a kid in Alaska, because of the remoteness, we had to wait about a week after the original television air dates enjoyed by the Lower 48 to watch our shows. We didn't have live TV, including important ball games, but we didn't feel deprived, of course. We'd never known any different. My dad kept this delay to himself for a long time and used it to his advantage. He always placed nickel bets with us on the outcome of the Super Bowl or in which round Muhammad Ali would knock 'em out. We were convinced Dad was prophetic and emptied our pockets that way.

So by the time I settled down to watch *A Christmas Carol*, all of the decorations had been packed and stored under Dad's ammo reloading bench upstairs, the unadorned tree had been chopped up and used in the woodstove, and the turkey's wishbone was finally brittle enough after sitting on the windowsill to provide a satisfying snap.

I guess the Christmas spirit had already passed, too, because I didn't enjoy watching perhaps the most famous Christmas story of all time (the most famous, after the original, of course). Ghosts, mean men, a neglected handicapped child . . . What's not to love? I must've been too young to handle the classic tale, because the story of stingy old Ebenezer Scrooge and fragile young Tiny Tim has definitely grown on me since. I even have a favorite line, which comes right after Ebenezer's dramatic change of heart following his encounter with the spirits:

"And it was always said of him, that he knew how to keep Christmas well," Dickens wrote, " . . . if any man alive possessed the knowledge. May that be truly said of us, and all of us."

I love that phrase "keeping Christmas well."

In the last chapter, I mentioned a few businesses that "keep Christmas well." I love proprietors who fearlessly celebrate Christmas even while other stores feel obligated to cower behind ambiguous holiday generalizations. But honoring Christmas is good for the community, makes financial sense, and is the right thing to do. Once again, it's not even that hard. Here are some general guidelines for small business owners on how to "keep Christmas well."

First, your business can reflect your community's values and traditions. As Sam Walton, the wildly successful founder of Wal-Mart, said:

"Each Wal-Mart store should reflect the values of its customers and support the vision they hold for their community."

Honoring your community isn't just good for business; it's the right thing to do. Obviously attracting patronage keeps food on your table, puts your kids through college, and lets you take that vacation.

Some people—like those angry atheists—say it's not "inclusive" to say "Merry Christmas" or to celebrate the season as it is. But here's a news flash: In a democracy, within a republic, nothing is ever completely "inclusive."

Since you're always going to offend somebody, you might as well do what's right.

Second, realize there are actually very few haters and cranks.

My dad always said the squeaky wheel gets the grease. That's why angry atheists and secular liberals get an inordinate amount of attention when they raise objections to just about anything—especially when the LSM agrees with and broadcasts their critique of a faith-filled populace. What ends up happening is the negative comments of a small group end up gaining a lot more momentum. This is true generally in life, but especially true in social media and the Internet. Have you ever read a good online article, only to see hundreds, if not thousands, of combative comments under the posting?

When I post something on Facebook, for example, you wouldn't believe the angry, outraged, and just plain silly and rude responses that immediately follow. And that doesn't even touch on the vile tweets people fire off. Does that mean a huge percentage of readers dislike what I write? I honestly don't think so.

An editor of the newspaper the *Guardian*, which has one of the most widely read British websites (widely read in America, too), recently revealed that their website publishes around 600,000 comments every single month beneath their articles, but that 2,600 people posted more than 40 comments per month. That's a lot of commenting by a relatively small number of readers. People started crunching those numbers to figure out just how representative those commenters were of the *Guardian*'s general readership. Quickly, they concluded that only 0.0037 percent of their audience actually takes the time to comment on an article. Martin

Belam crunched the numbers and explained, "The people who leave comments every day are very much *the statistical edge case*. They may be the main users of *the existing comment system*, but they are not the main users of *the site*."

Good phrase, the "statistical edge." That is just a nice way of saying there aren't many of them. They're fringe. Just like the customers who might complain about being wished a "Merry Christmas" when they don't believe in Christmas. While they may be vocal, they aren't expressing a sentiment representative of most customers' experiences or beliefs.

Small business owners, let this be a lesson. Don't be intimidated by this tiny minority. Just because they're loud, doesn't mean they're right.

You might be surprised at what happens when you stand up to the vocal few. For years, Americans have watched business after business cave every Christmas in the face of angry atheists and other liberals. Little did folks know, millions of American were literally hungry for a business to stand up for its values. Hungry enough to eat all the food in the store. Which brings me to my third point: Serve your customers well, and they'll stick with you when you stick to your principles.

Something amazing happened in the summer of 2012 when Chick-fil-A president Dan Cathy was asked a question about same-sex marriage: He answered from his heart. "I think we are inviting God's judgment on our nation when we shake our fist at Him and say, 'We know better than you as to what constitutes a marriage,'" he said. Later a Baptist newspaper published another quote from Cathy. "We are very much supportive of the family—the biblical definition of the family unit. . . . We know that it might not be popular with everyone, but, thank the Lord, we live in a country where we can share our values and operate on biblical principles."

Or so he thought he lived in that kind of country.

His comments set off a firestorm, but were his opinions that surprising? He was a Baptist church member, held prayer meetings at his restaurants, and the restaurants are closed on Sundays so employees can "have an opportunity to rest, spend time with family and friends, and worship if they choose to do so." No one should feign shock and awe upon discovering that the Cathys were the kind of folks who would believe in the traditional definition of marriage (especially since this was—until very recently—a belief shared by Democratic leaders, including the president). But liberal activists and politicians went hysterical anyway.

The mayor of Boston proposed a Chick-fil-A ban, saying he wouldn't allow the company to open any franchises in Beantown "unless they open up their policies." A Chicago alderman vowed to block a second Chick-fil-A until they did a "complete 180." The mayor of San Francisco tweeted condescending criticism. Even the Jim Henson Company announced it would no longer provide kids' toys in the Chick-fil-A children's meals.

All of this in spite of the fact that Chick-fil-A serves really good fast food to all customers, treats its employees fairly regardless of their race, creed, color, gender, or—yes—sexual orientation, and merely asks that they do their jobs well, treat their customers right, and respond with a cheerful "my pleasure" as they serve those tasty waffle fries.

As unfair as it all was, we've seen company after company change policies after much less pressure. It seems that a critical news story and a nasty tweet or two is all it takes these days to change corporate policies all across America.

But there were signs of hope. When eighty thousand people signed a petition demanding publisher HarperCollins no longer provide Berenstain Bears books in Chick-fil-A kids' meals, they didn't bow to the pressure. The publisher (the same publisher smart enough to publish this book) instead responded, "We have a long history of diversity and inclusiveness and work tirelessly to protect the freedom of expression. It is not our practice to cancel a contract with an author, or any other party, for exercising their First Amendment rights." Freedom of the press was alive and well at HarperCollins headquarters.

This was encouraging evidence that not everyone was furious. When there was no sign Chick-fil-A would cave and change its policies, America decided to show its support. In August 2012, customers showed up en masse on Chick-fil-A Appreciation Day, one of the largest spontaneous rebellions against the LSM and the cultural elite that I can remember. (Note to self: if you want to start a movement, it helps if you ask folks to "sacrifice" by eating "mor' chiken" and biscuits.) Customers lined up for hours for their chance to order chicken sandwiches. Lines snaked around the restaurants multiple times, police were called in to handle the sudden flow of traffic to the restaurants, and stores ran out of food.

Sadly, there are no Chick-fil-A restaurants in Alaska. So when I went to Texas around that time to rally for Senator Ted Cruz's campaign, Todd, Piper, and I knew exactly where we wanted to eat. On the way to the airport, we made sure we could swing by the Chick-fil-A in the Woodlands to grab a sandwich. We met an adorable little dance troupe inside raising money for their organization. The girls had a "wheel of fortune," which I got to spin. I won a biscuit, and that honey-drenched treat was as good as Mom's.

What did we learn? The public is starving for high-quality businesses that also honor the community's values—and don't retreat from a fight. That fun evening at Chick-fil-A with the dance troupe didn't feel political at all. It was just a great community coming together to support the restaurant by eating good food. Funny, not one person we encountered in there had politics on their minds. They were all there just to eat, socialize, and get people to spin a wheel of little pink tutu fortunes.

Of course, the media didn't quite cover it that way. They swept the amazing success under the rug, while promoting a "same-sex kiss-in" that turned out to be a gigantic flop. Those few customers who showed up to plant a big kiss on each other in the stores were greeted with . . . free drinks? Yep. All over the country, managers served the protesters by making sure they didn't get too overheated on the hot summer day.

"Blessed are you when people insult you, persecute you and falsely say all kinds of evil against you because of me" (Matthew 5:11).

Of course, there was little mention of the small turnout on network news.

Which brings me to my fourth and final point.

The media speaks for itself and not the masses. Ignore it.

I love seeing small business owners reload and take a stand to "keep Christmas well." But what about the rest of us? How can we personally keep it well, to the extent it's possible? Even though I've read those words from *A Christmas Carol* many times, I'm not sure I've quite figured it out. However, we do try.

Last year, on Christmas Eve, we all gathered around the fireplace and I had every intention of "keeping Christmas well." The Nativity story. A warm fire. Time with family. There are few things better. Just as I was about to open the book, however, I noticed Willow shooting Bristol a sideways glance. "Want to make a bet on how far she'll get before she starts bawling?"

"I'm not going to cry," I said. "I just . . ." But my protests fell flat.

Who was I kidding?

Normally, I never get emotional over sentimental things like this. I don't cry in movies (even *The Notebook*!). Nor am I the type of person who sees a commercial and get's teary. However, there's one glaring exception, and my family doesn't let me get away with it. Every year, I read " 'Twas the Night Before

Christmas" and then the story of the Nativity for the kids. And every year, the story of the birth of Christ chokes me up.

"Go on, Mom," Bristol urged. "We're listening." And then, to Willow, she said, "I'll give it to the no-room-at-the-inn part."

Todd dramatically took out his wallet and put a couple of dollars on the coffee table. "I'll give it to the wise men with the presents part."

Everyone laughed, and I knew they'd pegged me. Nevertheless, I cleared my throat and pushed on.

"Long ago, God sent an angel to a young Jewish woman named Mary and told her some surprising news . . ." As I read from the same children's book we read from every year, Trig, who was sitting in Todd's lap, pointed to the picture in the book. He loves to look at the pictures in a hardback book even more than swooshing images on the iPad, and seeing him interact with this story touched me. But I pressed on, trying to make it further into the story with my composure.

Christmas Eve is such a wonderful night, perhaps better than any other night of the year. It's the calm before the wrapping paper storm, when things are quiet and anticipation is high.

We always light tiny handheld candles and everyone in the extended family goes around the room to report what we're thankful for. Then I make the kids listen to me read these two stories. On our kitchen table, we place a candelabra and Hanukkah candles, as a way to acknowledge Christianity's Judeo-Christian roots.

See, I embrace diversity.

Okay. I confess I do tear up during the story of Jesus. (And don't play "Mary, Did You Know?" within earshot of me during Christmas if you're not carrying Kleenex.) But isn't the story great? I know, I know. We've heard it so many times at church it's like we've been inoculated against it. But I'd like to take just a moment and relish it:

A young married couple is expecting a baby under mysterious, and quite scandalous, circumstances. The husband, a carpenter, doesn't put his wife away, as some would have. Instead, he believes her story of a quite miraculous pregnancy, and they anxiously prepare for the arrival of their very special son. But there's one complication: The emperor orders everyone to go to their hometowns to be registered.

If the emperor wanted a census, it didn't matter you were about to give birth. The young, very pregnant mother hops up on a donkey and starts the long journey to Bethlehem. Once they arrive, of course, there's no place to stay. After being turned away by everyone they ask, they end up in a cattle stall. Let's just say it wouldn't have passed our health and safety standards for a sanitary place to give birth. Yet, this is where it happened . . . where the hope of the world arrived.

It gets me every time. Sometimes I'm asked to read my favorite Christmas story on local radio, and I invariably choose this one and blubber through it.

Last year, after I choked through the story, the kids selected one present from under the tree to open. We call these the "before Santa comes that night" gifts, and everyone takes great care to select the package that holds the most promise.

When Dickens encouraged us to "keep Christmas well," he might have been thinking of these types of annual traditions. The hot cocoa, the gifts, the parties, and Eskimo Bingo definitely play their part in making Christmas a festive, meaningful occasion.

But for Ebenezer, keeping Christmas well involved a major change of heart. Instead of being selfish, he was generous. Instead of being resentful, he was full of joy. He also began treating his employees more fairly and was described as "good a friend, as good a master, and as good a man as the good old City knew, or any other good old city, town, or borough in the good old world."

"Keeping Christmas well" had to do with his pretty significant change of heart. Now, I doubt any of us felt as terribly toward Christmas as Ebenezer originally did, as when he said, "Every idiot who goes about with 'Merry Christmas' on his lips should be boiled with his own pudding, and buried with a stake of holly through his heart." However, many of us do think of Christmas as an inconvenience or a costly diversion from the normal pattern of life. I've sometimes let my December calendar get too full, so that what should be a peaceful time with the family becomes a rushed effort to get everything on my to-do list accomplished. We've all been there. But let's learn a lesson from the first person to really deal with Christmas: Mary herself. After the angel came and told her that she was going to have a baby, Luke records:

> *But Mary kept all these things, and pondered them*
> *in her heart.*
>
> —LUKE 2:19

So, Mary "kept Christmas well" by keeping the idea of her son in her heart. She pondered the mystery surrounding his arrival. She probably held his tiny hand, wondering who he was . . . not realizing one day that hand would be pierced. She already knew His birth had changed her life, but maybe she contemplated how it would change other people's lives as well. Christmas exists in the actual event of the birth of Christ, so we should also pause to ponder his life, its effect on us, and what effect we should have on other people.

Here's a story to show you how:

Every year, we have the annual Wasilla Community Christmas Dinner, a tradition that began when former mayor Newcomb partnered with a local restaurateur to serve some turkeys to almost a hundred people at our local senior citizens center. They had so much fun, they made it an annual tradition. Over the past twenty-two years, the number of people served has grown so much that the event was moved to the high school and then to our local hockey rink. This is due, at least in part, to the fact that many people find themselves alone at Christmas in Alaska. Some don't have extended family in our state, while others have loved ones who work on North Slope oil field schedules or far out of town in their resource development jobs.

My mom, dad, and their friends have been instrumental in helping put on this wonderful community-wide event. Last year, they served more than a hundred turkeys, five hundred pounds of ham, five hundred pounds of prime rib, four hundred and fifty pounds of carrots, seven hundred pounds of potatoes, and hundreds of deliciously prepared homemade desserts donated from people of the Mat-Su (Matanuska-Susitna) borough.

But one year was a little less festive than normal. In 2008, the mashed potatoes had never smelled better, as we scooped out spoonful after spoonful to the diners. The high school cafeteria had been transformed into a festive Christmas atmosphere . . . with the addition of green to the Wasilla Warriors' red and white. People volunteered for all sorts of activities to make the day special. They cooked potatoes and peeled carrots in the home-ec room, delivered food to shut-ins, wrapped presents, and cleaned. My dear friend Theresa Nelson, my teenage daughter Bristol, and I were on the serving line that year, and we were in charge of one of the more popular items. It was another amazing Christmas with my community.

But still.

It didn't feel right.

As I stood there, wearing a red apron and a smile, I ached inside. I watched as my good friend so lovingly offered food and fellowship, to one person after another. But under her smile, I knew she was in pain. What the people filing through our line didn't realize was that her husband had just recently died of a heart attack.

And yet she served.

As I stood next to my teenage daughter, I knew she was experiencing many emotions, too. I watched her scoop out the potatoes and place a warm mound on an older gentleman's plate, but I knew it was hard for her to be there. My child—she was just a baby—was about to become a mother herself. No doubt she wasn't looking at those red-and-white Warriors walls through the same eyes as other students who helped out that day. Her life was about to change forever.

And yet she served.

There's something about the Christmas season that makes everyone feel like heading out to the soup kitchen. Last year, Americans collectively gave billions, a great percentage of which came in between Thanksgiving and New Year's Eve. Kids at church frequently pick "angels" from Christmas trees to give presents to; moms pack shoe boxes of goodies for kids in faraway countries; my family and I worked with Samaritan's Purse in warm Haiti and joined local Salvation Army volunteers freezing in Alaska as they stood outside stores, hoping for extra change in their kettles. When Americans "get their Christmas on," it sometimes looks like shopping till they drop. But frequently, this shopping is for other people—children they'll never meet, parents who need a helping hand, or for organizations that provide assistance all year.

I bet Charles Darwin never understood this. If the world could be described as truly "survival of the fittest," why would people collectively be stricken with a spirit of generosity in December? Why would parents worried about braces, college, and taxes suddenly write a check for victims of hurricanes or tsunamis? Why would children empty their piggy banks for orphans in need, even if it meant they'd do without their new baseball gloves, bicycles, or the coolest new clothes?

It doesn't make sense.

Unless.

Perhaps there really is a "spirit" associated with Christmas. Frequently called "Christmas cheer"—as in the funny movie *Elf*—there might be something more to it than warm feelings associated with the gifts, the Bing Crosby songs, and the smell of pine wafting through the house on chilly December mornings. Maybe the echo of God's generosity rings in each of our hearts, regardless of whether we're concerned about that baby in the manger or realize where that spirit that tugs at our hearts originates.

But on that day in the Warriors high school cafeteria, it was no mystery to me.

It had been fewer than two months since John McCain and I had lost the election to Barack Obama and Joe Biden (coming in second, out of two). I'd been through a challenging campaign for the vice presidency in which I'd been maligned, my family had been mocked, my e-mail had been hacked, and our privacy lost. There was literally no accusation against us that was too strange, too bizarre, to publish. After I returned to Juneau, we finished the legislative session and I was entering my "lame duck" legislative year as governor.

There were even more pressing concerns. Track was headed to combat in the Diyala Province of Iraq. I was so proud of his patriotism and his sense of duty, but I worried. At the same time, we had a scare with my other son, Trig. During this time, we believed he needed majorly intrusive open-heart surgery to repair the holes in his tiny, infant heart. Thankfully, the holes mended without the assistance of a surgical team, and his heart was made whole. (Thank you, God.) Mine, however, was heavy and troubled as we tried to sort through his health issues, Track's upcoming departure, and Bristol's pregnancy. Plus, after the campaign, I was ready to take my governing responsibilities very seriously—as always since the Last Frontier's plate was very full. But when I returned, I was slammed with ridiculous charges (some charges so hilarious they actually gave participating lawyers a bad name), costing millions of dollars and most hours of my days. We were shackled by lawsuit after lawsuit. For the sake of my state, I wasn't going to let them win. However, the situation thwarted my ability to move the state forward. My approval ratings—which had been the highest in the nation—plummeted. My heart has always been—and is—full of love for Alaska. But during that Christmas, it was heavy. I was stuck in a situation unfair to my family and to the hardworking Alaskans whom I served.

And yet, spooning out the potatoes at the high school cafeteria somehow soothed my soul. With each person coming through my line, I felt my heart become lighter and less burdened. The whole scenario reminded me of Psalm 123, which partly reads, "So our eyes look to the Lord our God, till he shows us his mercy. Have mercy on us, Lord, have mercy on us, for we have endured no end of contempt."

The Psalmist was in a bad spot, so he pleaded for mercy. Mercy. That's the essence of the Christmas spirit, isn't it? It's often a cliché to say that the best way to keep Christmas well is to "serve others," but clichés are usually grounded in truth. We serve because we know we need mercy, too.

The apostle Paul wrote, "I will glory in my infirmity for when I am weak, then I am strong."

Tough times show us that we need a Savior. At least that's how I felt that year, serving warm meals to people in need in our community. I smiled at the folks smiling back as they went through the line, listened to the giggles of little children opening the community-provided presents, and realized how much we all need mercy.

From God. From each other. From ourselves.

The Christmas spirit has been described in many ways, but mercy is a big part of it. In fact, the Christmas story is a lot grittier than the Christmas television specials would have you believe. New York City pastor Tim Keller tried to illustrate this "grittiness" by explaining a fundamental aspect of relationships. (Pay attention, starry-eyed newlyweds.) All people eventually disappoint. No matter how awesome your friends or family are, something eventually goes wrong and that is when we need mercy the most.

"Something went wrong," as Keller suggested, earlier that year in my own family. Months before the Wasilla Community Christmas Dinner and long before we knew the outcome of the election. What "went wrong" had nothing to do with politics and was much more personal. I had just given birth to Trig, who arrived early, and I was attending a sweet baby shower my friend had thrown. My Wasilla girlfriends were all there. Because I'd been back in the state capitol—where Trig slept in my governor's office under our state flag, emblazoned with the Great North Star—this was the first time Trig met the special women in my life. We had such a wonderful time all kicked back on a warm, soft, carpeted living room floor while we cooed in Trig's ear and passed him around, warm arms to arms, heart to heart.

"He's beautiful," my friends said.

My spirit soared. I had a sense of homecoming and peace as a friend sang a song of God's grace to my baby, then sang to all of us as we all silently acknowledged a new chapter in our circle's life. It was a serene afternoon, when everyone felt "right" with the world.

I was very content when I got home that spring day and my sisters helped me put up all Trig's presents. After they left, Todd went to his shop to assemble one of the best gifts ever—a baby jogger with fat treaded tires so I could lull the baby to sleep on my laboriously slow runs along paths partially circling Juneau's blue waters and calving glaciers, in rain, sleet, *and* snow. I was thumbing through the maintenance manual, so excited to get back outdoors and back to normal, when Bristol stopped me dead in my tracks. She'd been at the shower, but she suddenly seemed upset.

"We need to talk," she said. She was sitting with her boyfriend and another friend. I sat down across from the three teens. Todd joined me. He wasn't smiling. Willow was eavesdropping upstairs.

"You aren't getting a truck." I laughed. "There's no way your job at the coffee shack will pay for it."

"Mom," she said. "This is serious."

"What is it?" Todd asked.

That's when Bristol began sobbing. She didn't exactly tell us that she was pregnant. Eventually, her friend had to break the news to us when it was obvious that we'd never find out the news if we were waiting on Bristol's composure.

"Are you kidding?" I said. That was my first reaction, and I regret it to this day.

"Mom," Bristol wailed. "Why would I be crying if this was all a big joke?"

She had a point. My mind was reeling, so I sat down in a chair and blurted out the next thing that came to mind.

"Okay," I said, looking at Bristol and her boyfriend. "So when are you getting married?"

"Whoa, whoa, whoa," Todd said. "Not so fast."

"What do you mean, 'not so fast'?" I said. Our little world seemed to abruptly stop spinning, but at the same time a million thoughts and senses rushed me and landed right between my eyes. So much for getting everything back to normal.

"Come here, Sarah, please," he said as he got up and walked the few feet to our bedroom door. "We need to talk privately." His tone didn't sound like he was merely requesting me to follow. As soon as our bedroom door shut, I wheeled around at Todd and gave him the full brunt of my shock.

"What's wrong with you?" I asked.

"With me?" he responded. Trig was asleep in the middle of our bed, encircled with soft blue pillows and a hand-stitched yellow baby blanket. The other kids were outside playing. It was one of the first warm days of the year. "Since when did this become about me?"

"You're going to just casually dismiss the idea of marriage?" I said. "Right in front of the kids?" Even verbalizing the situation—talking about a baby and a wedding for people I still called "the kids" made me wince. "They need to get married and raise this baby together, and I can't *believe* you could argue against this. What is wrong with you?" I repeated.

Todd replied, "We already have a problem. I'm trying to stop you from adding more problems to Bristol's plate."

"Oh, that's rich," I said. "Really nice."

"I'm not saying you're *trying* to make it worse," he said.

"But you're saying I *am* making it worse? I'm her mother," I said. "I'm trying to help, but you're oh-so-willing to let them skirt away their responsibility." I'm not sure why I said that. Todd Palin is all about responsibility. Not only is he a commercial fisherman; he's owned outdoor recreation and property development businesses, he worked full-time for years as a production operator in the North Slope oil fields, coached the kids' teams, is still hands-on Mr. Mom as he's assisted every venture I've ever undertaken, promoting vo-tech curriculums in our school while serving as Alaska's First Gentleman (or as constituents called him, "First Dude"). The man built our house and cabin, sleeps less than anyone I know, and is pretty legendary—and not only because he's won the Iron Dog so many times. His first responsibility has always been family.

Probably because of the shock, but certainly because I was being unkind, I lit into him anyway. After many more sentences, he'd had enough. "You're wrong. Not only are you wrong to even insinuate our daughter should marry that . . ."

I waited and was surprised when he settled on the very descriptive yet neutral word ". . . boy. You're wrong to act like *I'm* the enemy."

On that spring day, which now seems a lifetime ago, Todd and I were so busy fighting we weren't even really talking about the issue at hand. Maybe because it was easier to focus on each other instead of the unwed pregnancy of our teenager, we stood in that room and bickered. After just a few minutes, even though I thought he was being pigheaded, I wanted him back. I wanted things to be okay between us, for our marriage to even thrive through this turmoil. So, instead of tying up my shoelaces and taking a jog—one of the ways I blow off steam—I looked straight into his eyes and saw an enormous amount of pain.

Not only was there disappointment over the situation, but there was hurt in his eyes over the way I'd immediately turned on him in my shock. I suddenly realized the truth. We'd been together since high school. Married for more than twenty years by this time, I could tell he wasn't even sure exactly what to do. But I suddenly sensed the character of Todd Palin again. He was forward-looking, practical, and protective. I could see it was manifesting in his insistence that Bristol make her own decision about getting married . . . even though he was confident it would be a mistake.

"You're right," I finally said. Then I added a barely audible, "I'm sorry."

When things "go wrong," as Pastor Keller explained, it's all too easy to bicker and point fingers. Todd wouldn't budge when he thought I was giving bad advice, and I wasn't going to make any concession to him, either.

"You're to blame."

"No, it's your fault."

"No, you."

I know Todd and I aren't unique. If relationships are real, they'll run into problems. However, something amazing happens if, as Keller suggests, you show mercy.

"You're to blame!"

"No, it's your fault!"

"Okay, it's me."

When I finally realized I needed to take the blame on that day, Todd's face instantly softened toward me. There's something remarkable that happens when one person bridges the ever-widening gap by taking the blame and becoming vulnerable. The relationship suddenly has a chance. Both people can let their defenses down. That one sentence, "Yeah, I'm to blame," even makes the relationship stronger.

Mercy stuck by us Christmas of that year. About half a year after Bristol broke the news of her pregnancy to us, she stood by my side as we served up hot food to those in need. When we returned home after the Wasilla Community Christmas Dinner, Bristol held Trig for me all afternoon, as I wrapped up an interview and then finally kicked off my shoes to play with Piper and her cousins near the tree. My parents and Todd's parents arrived with blueberry and pumpkin pies and punch ingredients, as five generations of family bustled around the kitchen putting together a feast. There are never enough chairs, so the little kids sat on benches near the buffet of traditional dishes spread around the counters, the big kids reached over them to fill their plates, a bunch of the guys had television trays in front of holiday ball games, and two lace-covered tables hosted those who chose a more formal family potluck. After my mom prayed over the guests and the meal, I encouraged everyone to eat slowly.

"Christmas Day goes by too quickly," I said. "So take your time."

However, I could tell that people were already busy eating, laughing, and chatting. We ate lots of food that day, and finally cleared dishes so we could move tables together to make room for Eskimo Bingo.

Bristol did her best to join the rowdy crew sitting in a circle exchanging secret gifts as the timer ticked away and noise levels and intensity rose. I caught her eye throughout the evening. She tried to keep a smile on her face, with a warm embrace around her baby brother the entire evening, but she could not feign the glee that everyone else exuded. She rubbed her lower back and I saw her chin quiver. I moved over next to her, kissed Trig's sleepy face, and put my hand on her back. Her eyes began to fill and she whispered that she didn't feel well at all.

In just a few hours, her labor pains began.

She gave birth to Tripp Easton Mitchell two days later.

I held my grandson for the first time in the local hospital where my own son was born just eight months earlier. When Bristol's son arrived, he melted into our arms and melted my heart. My little girl had given life to this little boy. In less than ideal circumstances, he turned our little world upside down . . . for the better.

Mercy, I thought, as I looked at the seven-pound, seven-ounce bundle. He was so helpless, so vulnerable. Isn't it astonishing that two millennia ago, God came in the most fragile of vessels, an infant?

As Pastor Keller said, "In the gift of Christmas, the unassailable, omnipotent God became a baby, giving us the ultimate example of letting our defenses down."

He didn't have to come as an infant. This has to be one of the most incredibly counterintuitive moves ever recorded in the Bible. "That's one of the reasons I believe Christianity," wrote one of my favorite authors, C. S. Lewis. "It's a religion you couldn't have guessed."

Of course, showing mercy is painful. I confess, I didn't like to admit that Todd was right about not encouraging Bristol to be linked maritally to her high school boyfriend at the time, but he definitely was. Time would tell.

"It hurts, but it's the only way," Keller said about reconciliation, because "it's a costly act of redemption for the relationship. And it works because we are created in the image of the One who gave the ultimate expression of this part of his own nature at Christmas."

Keller then quotes from C. S. Lewis, from *The Four Loves*.

> *To love at all is to be vulnerable. Love anything, and your heart will certainly be wrung and possibly be broken. If you want to make sure of keeping it intact, you must give your heart to no one, not even to an animal. Wrap it carefully round with hobbies and little luxuries; avoid all entanglements; lock it up safe in the casket or coffin of your selfishness. But in that casket—safe, dark, motionless, airless—it will change. It will not be broken; it will become unbreakable, impenetrable, irredeemable.*

If you live and love in this world, you'll be hurt. Which is why this whole manger thing is so, well, astonishing. God came as a tiny, breakable baby instead of a conquering king. He came as a baby needing care. He came as someone we could damage and hurt.

Why would a King lower himself into this very strange, helpless position?

Because He wanted to make things good between us. He wanted us back and was willing to take the blame. How amazing is it that He was willing to take the blame upon himself, when He never had even done anything wrong. In my story, I was blinded by shock and fear when I began to treat Todd poorly. Jesus was willing to lower Himself and become vulnerable even though He wasn't actually at fault.

No, the Christmas story isn't really "magical." It's not the holiday version of Disneyland, polished and shined up for people to walk admiringly through before getting to the gift shop. No, Christmas is grit, it's mercy, it's vulnerability.

If we really internalized its message, we'd be free to be honest about our failures and shortcomings. We'd finally be relieved of the pressure of impressing each other with our own goodness. It would allow us to embrace our "inner cattle stall," to admit it when we do wrong, to accept forgiveness, and to face any hardship that comes our way.

And I'd argue *that* is what Christmas is all about, and our culture needs more of that.

Not less.

I always love to have all the kids around during Christmas. This is the crew in 2005—check out Todd's Tom Selleck mustache!

5

Bad News, Good News

*This is no time to engage in the luxury
of cooling off or to take the tranquilizing
drug of gradualism.*

—MARTIN LUTHER KING, JR.

Southeastern University is located in Lakeland, Florida, and they have one of the best mascots in the country. Instead of a cardinal perched on a limb or a rocket spiraling into space, its mascot is fire. A flame, interwoven in its name and onto uniforms, representing the school's mission and ideals. Often a name is providential, not just coincidental. I was delighted to accept Southeastern's invitation to speak on campus at its Leadership Forum in March. It made me smile to think I would literally be "under fire" that day. Not only would I be allowed free rein to address any topic, but— through follow-up interviews and a Q&A session—I'd be able to share a most important message with their students. In whatever minuscule way I could, I wanted to encourage and empower them.

It didn't hurt, either, that Florida was one hundred degrees warmer than frigid Fairbanks, where we had recently trekked to cheer Todd across the Iron Dog finish line on the frozen Chena River. I was happy to head south to thaw out, so I exchanged Bunny Boots for a pair of Bristol's heels and headed down to Lakeland.

During my speech, I recited one of my favorite quotes to the students, faculty, and Southeastern supporters: "We in this country, in this generation, are—by destiny rather than choice—the watchmen on the walls of world freedom. We ask, therefore, that we may be worthy of our power and responsibility, that we may exercise our strength with wisdom and restraint, and that we may achieve in our time and for all time the ancient vision of 'peace on earth, goodwill toward men.' That must always be our goal, and the righteousness of our cause must always underlie our strength. For as was written long ago: 'except the Lord keep the city, the watchman waketh but in vain.' "

The source of this quote? Which right-wing pundit called America the "watchman on the walls" for the world? What radical televangelist just had to add a Bible verse in there for good measure?

The answer might surprise you. The above quote would be ridiculously polarizing in today's über-partisan culture—if a Republican leader uttered it, I could easily imagine the "talking heads" on television immediately dissecting it:

"What does it mean our country is a nation 'of destiny'?"

"How patronizing to call ourselves the 'watchmen' of the world."

"Since when did America begin to have the market on 'righteousness'?"

"So now the whole country has to be kept by 'the Lord'? Whose Lord?"

What my audience may not have known is that the above words are excerpted from a speech John F. Kennedy was scheduled to deliver on November 22, 1963. Tragically, he never got to the podium that day, because he was assassinated in Dallas en route in his motorcade. Years later, his prepared remarks were released to the public, and we were finally able to see the significant message he intended to deliver that fateful day.

I especially love JFK's quote from Psalm 127:

Except the Lord keep the city, the watchman waketh but in vain.

Kennedy was going to invoke God's protection on our country so that we might live up to our responsibility in the world. "Fifty years later, as a nation, do we still even believe that the Lord should 'keep the city'?" I asked the Leadership Forum. "Have we forgotten God altogether? Are we watchmen waking 'but in vain'?"

There in Dallas, before many of us were even born, the president crafted a speech, keeping notes in a folder, jotting thoughts on note cards, and writing ideas he planned to deliver to the Dallas Citizens Council. Though they never heard his speech, I believe JFK's message was providentially recorded for teaching and encouraging today. If we listened to his speech—and really took it to heart—it would answer many of America's challenges.

Our Founders understood the vital importance of morality and faith in preserving our republic. Our second president, John Adams—who was present at most every key moment in the formation of our nation—wrote, "Our Constitution was made only for a moral and religious people. It is wholly inadequate to the government of any other."

The Constitution alone, great document that it is, is not enough to hold us together without something within our own moral character as a people. Its governing principles are the best protection against tyranny, but they won't assure the survival of liberty. Words written on a document simply aren't enough to sustain us. Freedom is, above all, a question of culture and of the morals in which a culture is grounded.

It's just common sense: A democracy reflects the culture and values of its people. An example is another democracy in the world: Egypt after the so-called Arab Spring. After generations of dictators, the people there had a choice, and they chose the Muslim Brotherhood. They chose a government that enacted a Sharia-based constitution, oppresses Christians, and imprisons dissenters. Why? Because that level of intolerance is widely represented in Egyptian culture. A recent Pew poll showed that the vast majority of Egyptians not only support Sharia law (which includes suppression of women's rights and independence), they support executing people who convert from Islam. Thankfully, the Egyptian people reconsidered their support for the Muslim Brotherhood and threw them out of office after a popular uprising, but the jury is still out on that country's fragile political system.

A democracy without respect for individual liberty is just a tyranny of the majority. The right to vote doesn't guarantee virtue. The point is, freedom is the only answer.

Thankfully, we're not Egypt, but what are today's national trends in America? Are Americans emphasizing the values that made our nation great, or are we rejecting them? If we reject those values, what kind of nation will we create?

Well, we're building our nation, every day, one young citizen at a time. There, amid the Fire, I wanted to spark a flame under any young citizen independent and strong enough to forge through the mockery and criticism from a society that rejects the traditional American values so eloquently described by the likes of John F. Kennedy and John Adams.

If our schools are the centers of influence, directing our collective path by molding the citizens of the future, we can get a good glimpse of where we're headed by taking a look at American students. Take your typical sixth-grader; we'll call him Joe the Student.

"Please explain what you did on winter break in six hundred words or less," the teacher wrote on the dry-erase board one afternoon. When twelve-year-old Joey got his paper back, he'd made a 95.

"Not bad," his mother said the following day as she was looking through the weekly homework folder. "What did you miss?"

Joey grabbed the paper from his mom's hand and groaned. "She counted off because I called it 'Christmas Break,' instead of 'Winter Break,'" he explained, noticing the red writing in perfect cursive at the top of the page. "Oh, my teacher wrote, 'Pay attention to the language in the assignment on the board. "Winter" is the more inclusive term we use at school.'"

His mom took a sip of coffee and sighed. "It's okay," she said. "Just pay attention to the assignment next time," she reminded him before signing the folder and slipping it back into her son's backpack.

Is that a small matter? Insignificant? Do we just roll our eyes, sigh—like the mother did in the story—and move on?

No. Absolutely not. What happened in that story is important, and here's why.

Our children are growing up in a culture where faith is regularly stigmatized. Through their word choices, our educators relentlessly tell us that some religions are worth honoring while others must be suppressed, mentioned mainly in the home. Kids get the message.

It's time we open our eyes and see the chilling effects that this stigmatizing political correctness has had on religion in general.

In Joey's case above, something was lost, and it was much more significant than five points off a homework grade. Joey may have learned to pay closer attention to what the teacher writes on the dry-erase board, but he also learned there must be something wrong—even offensive—about the word "Christmas." Since he's only in the sixth grade, it might take more for him to *really get it*. However, the lesson—that words with religious connotations should not be uttered in front of nonreligious friends—will be impressed on him time and time again. Over the course of his life in school, his teachers may not necessarily make sure he knows how to spell or do arithmetic (and if some strong-armed, union-dominated public schools don't change, his chances to learn basic math diminish by the year), but they will certainly try to shape his views of Christianity.

Joey is a talented singer, so when the school's "Winter Pageant" comes up that December, he's asked to sing a solo. He chooses his song, practices in his garage, and nervously prepares to debut it in front of his choir teacher.

"Sorry," the music teacher says the next day, after he has had time to review the selections. "Joey, you'll need to pick a different song. 'Little Drummer Boy' just won't do."

"What's wrong with it?" he asks. The song was the one he'd selected because he'd recently become a Christian at summer camp, and the song celebrates his faith's humble foundation.

"You notice, young man, that not everyone around here believes in God," the teacher says curtly. "Just pick something that won't make other students uncomfortable."

Joey grabs his backpack and heads home, a little embarrassed.

"Mom," he says, "we have to pick a new song."

Mom puts away her paperwork, goes on the Internet, and starts looking for a more acceptable song choice. They settle on "Let It Snow! Let It Snow! Let It Snow!" Though Joey can't muster much sincere enthusiasm for the old classic, he's relieved that they found a song with more universally enjoyable lyrics.

Once again, he's learned a lesson: There's something wrong with sharing faith in public. But the school system is not done with him yet. Far from it.

Middle school is an anxious and a bit bizarre time for any kid. On the morning of abbreviated orientation classes, Joey settles into his desk and meets his homeroom teacher.

"Okay, class," Mr. Morris says, trying to acclimate the new kids to the school. "Every morning, we'll do the same thing: listen to announcements, collect any permission slips, stand for the Pledge of Allegiance, and you'll have about ten minutes to sit quietly at your desk before first period."

Joey had transferred into this new charter school and didn't know any of the students, most of whom had been going here since kindergarten. Then, with a smile, he notices one of the girls sitting in the front row also attended his former elementary school. Before he can catch her eye, the loudspeaker crackles to life.

The principal announces wrestling, soccer, and basketball tryouts all are happening that very week. Joey swallows hard as he wonders what basketball skills the tryouts would require. He is reprimanding himself for not working on his vertical all summer when quickly everyone stands for the Pledge of Allegiance. "If you do not wish to join with us as a matter of conscience," the principal says in a monotone, "you do not have to say the Pledge." Everyone stands, except a guy in the back who is listening to his iPod.

"I pledge allegiance . . . to the flag . . . of the United States of America," the class says in unison.

Joe's lips move but his mind is reeling. Maybe he should wait out fall sports and just try out for hockey instead. He feels he lacks finesse so figures he'll master enforcement in the corners and be able to make the team, he is thinking. These kinds of decisions will set his social circles for the rest of middle school.

"And to the republic for which it stands," he says, as he asks himself, "What would Scotty Gomez do? What would Mike Fisher advise?" "One nation . . . under God . . . indivis—"

Joey stops cold. For some reason, a few of his classmates turn and snicker. Did he belch without realizing it? Did he do something wrong? Thankfully, the bell rings, which lets him bolt out the door. He is stopped when the teacher grabs his arm.

"Excuse me," Mr. Morris says. "What is your name?"

Joey watches as his friend slips out the door before he can catch her.

"I'm Joey," he says quickly. Has he already gotten in trouble?

"You're new here?" Mr. Morris asks, but the intimidated twelve-year-old can tell by the condescending look on the teacher's face that he already

knew. "I heard you say the Pledge of Allegiance, and we do things differently here at this school."

"What do you mean?" Joey asks. He's been saying the Pledge his entire school life. It was one thing he assumed he didn't have to relearn.

"Well, at this school, we don't say the words 'under God,'" the instructor says in a lowered voice. "It makes some of the nonreligious students feel excluded. Besides, do you think God only blesses America? I'm sure you understand, kiddo."

Joey doesn't know how to get to his first period class, and fears he'll be late.

"Sure," he says. "Sorry," before rushing out the classroom, and making a mental note to remember for the next homeroom. "One nation . . . indivisible," he practices as he rushes through the hallways alone. "What the heck? I have to remember that."

If you think these examples are purely fictitious, think again. There are schools across the nation that have removed the "under God" line from the Pledge. Independence Charter in Philadelphia voluntarily removed the line to make students of no faith feel more comfortable. An atheist family sued Acton-Boxborough Regional School District in Massachusetts to get them to stop saying the entire Pledge, saying that it was unfair to the atheist students who didn't want to even hear it.

You don't need more proof that schools all over America have renamed Christmas Break.

But what about the song choice being vetoed because of its religious nature? That happened, too, when a little girl in California who wanted to sing "Beneath the Waters (I Will Rise)," a song about baptism. The school told her she had to pick another, non-religious song.

These stories are based on reality, so don't discount them because you think they're products of an overly active imagination. Our kids are growing up in a different climate than we did. And it's time to do something about it.

As you think through the above scenarios, here's something else to consider. Remember the Left pushes two contradictory ideas. First, they claim that words like "under God" and songs like "Little Drummer Boy" are so important (even dangerous) that they are justified in using the power of the state to censor them, filing federal lawsuits to have them removed from schools. But then the Left tells people of faith that we're silly for resisting these changes because these "unimportant" words and songs aren't really a core part of our "right to worship." Well, which is it?

You would've known the answer even if I hadn't told you my tragic-at-the-time Sony Walkman story. Words matter. Our Founding Fathers knew that, too. These words form the ideas that shape our values and describe what it means to be of good character.

When John Adams wrote, "Our Constitution was made only for a moral and religious people. It is wholly inadequate to the government of any other," he understood that a healthy republic, and indeed, all healthy governments, are grounded in moral principles that we learn through the philosophical and religious forms of reasoning. And how are these forms of reasoning expressed? Through words. We are first introduced to them through words before they are incorporated into how we live our lives.

So are you ready for some good old-fashioned words? Here are some: work, honesty, courage, justice, thrift, perseverance. Here are some phrases: "respect for life" and "love thy neighbor." These words and phrases are actually values that sustain a healthy republic. Without these values, our Constitution won't hold us together, because we won't hold to our Constitution.

Already we see the strain from our lost values. Our federal government has become a bankrupt, bloated, corrupt, out-of-control mess. Our leaders know this, and yet refuse to take action to correct course.

Consider the fact that Congress hasn't passed a budget in years, in spite of the fact that Article I, Section 9, clause 7 of the Constitution states: "No Money shall be drawn from the Treasury, but in Consequence of Appropriations made by Law; and a regular Statement and Account of the Receipts and Expenditures of all public Money shall be published from time to time." Our government must pass a budget; it's not just mandated—it's common sense to allow "We the People" to see our government's priorities and blueprint for the future, and it lets us hold our politicians accountable. Pretty simple. The liberal press inexplicably disagrees. And yet *I'm* pegged the idiot by the LSM?

Our federal government has been chugging along for years in violation of this basic clause in our Constitution. Again, our Constitution won't hold us together when we won't hold to our Constitution.

Even worse, as the moral fabric of our country frays, we turn to the government to make up for our personal failings. Yet we can't print enough currency or food stamps or free Obamaphone vouchers to compensate for failing families. The government is not a good parent.

Many people see we're losing core values and regret it. But even if they are wringing their hands, they refuse to face the truth: True character comes from our Creator, not merely from the mind of man. Left to our own devices, without God in our lives, we drift toward evil. As I've noted, the world's most murderous regimes—from Nazi Germany, to Stalin's Russia, to Mao's China—shared either a ruthless atheism or an explicit rejection of traditional Judeo-Christian beliefs (or both).

Notably, Americans are rejecting established religion. According to some polls, the fastest-growing "religious" group in America is the "nones"—the people who reject any religious label at all. This isn't good for us individually, and it's certainly not good for us culturally. When we reject a common core faith, it is difficult to maintain a common character, to protect common values.

Take Joey, for example. Though he belonged to a Christian family, his parents didn't notice as the school and society gradually but certainly began poisoning their son with the unmistakable message that their faith was unmentionable . . . that good manners would dictate he change his message for the comfort of others . . . that society is better off without faith. His family is busy with life—getting to work on time, paying bills, fixing flat tires and leaky roofs and making sure Grandpa is eating right. They don't even realize that their boy has been contaminated by this seemingly innocuous message, though the poisonous message will gradually take hold.

It's understandable that parents don't want to resist, to push back at every slight or act of petty censorship. When you're trying to make ends meet, or struggling to get the kids to practice on time, or pounding the pavement looking for a job, the thought of taking on your child's school over a song can seem so exhausting. Yet we have to resist the idea that the temporary (our hectic schedules) can trump the eternal (our child's view of God).

America is a nation "under God," and it's worth fighting to tell that truth. The Left certainly thinks it's worth fighting to deny it.

A few years back I read a book that told a startling story about a suicidal person about to jump from San Francisco's Golden Gate Bridge, causing a traffic jam as the first responders tried to talk him down. While this was going on, some angry commuters started shouting, "Just jump!" This happened in arguably the most liberal city in America—the birthplace of the "Summer of Love," for crying out loud. Some of those "loving" citizens—who may think of Christians as hate-filled bigots—cared more about the convenience of their commute than a desperate man's life.

But we don't have to go all the way to California for examples of moral decay. Just flip on the television, take a walk around your kids' school, or—if you've got the guts—scroll through kids' text messages. The coarsening of our culture is evident everywhere, and we now have a generation of young people being raised in a culture where our Judeo-Christian heritage is mocked and reviled. Where we can't even say "Merry Christmas." The very notion that we *have* a Judeo-Christian heritage is under attack.

I'm not talking about the nuances in theology or the differences between denominations. I'm talking basic stuff like the Golden Rule, the Ten Commandments' prohibition on stealing, killing, and lying, and so forth. And sexual morality? The two words don't seem to go together anymore.

Previously, I wrote about how Peter Hitchens examined the Soviet Union during its moral collapse. But there are many historical examples of the results of an antagonism toward Christianity. Look at the French Revolution. The Jacobins were radical atheists who hated Christianity and wanted to completely demolish it. It was so bad that they were changing the street names in Paris to remove any reference to the saints. (We wouldn't want any Frenchman to be offended and have a totally rotten, ruined day after glancing up at road signs to find his favorite baguette shop.) They gradually demolished or took over the churches and monasteries, killing or imprisoning every priest and nun who wouldn't become a puppet for the state.

And what was the result? Utopia? No, the guillotine.

Of course, in America, we aren't nailing shut the churches, yanking the preachers from their pulpits and leading them to their death as they did during the French Revolution. But we are doing more than just asking a sixth-grader to choose a nonreligious song for the winter concert. In America today, we are killing unborn children at a catastrophic pace. Since *Roe v. Wade* was decided in 1973, the U.S. Centers for Disease Control and Prevention estimates, well over 50 million babies have been killed.

Our nation actually uses the power of the state to protect the "right" to kill children in a mother's womb—for any reason or no reason at all. Do we worship ourselves so much that another human has to die for our personal convenience? A culture that reveres our Creator and respects the sanctity of innocent life does not condone killing its own children.

But that should be merely the building block, the first principle of a virtuous society. Vibrant faith has other virtues as well.

First, it provides a check on the power of the state. There's a reason why voters don't necessarily like voting for an atheist. Voters don't want to give power to someone who doesn't believe he or she will some-day have to answer to the Ultimate Authority. Atheists might counter that a leader answers to the people, but we all know that leaders often usurp power and else-where have taken over governments. History shows us again and again that an attack on faith (in particular, Christianity) inevitably leads to an attack on the rights of the people. When we dictate our own morality, we are capable of anything. When we submit our lives to living in faith, then self-sacrificial love becomes the purpose of life itself.

Second, faith has been an amazing force for good in our culture. Dr. Thomas Sowell reviewed Adam Hochschild's book *Bury the Chains*, which discussed the world's first antislavery movement. Sowell writes:

The anti-slavery movement was spearheaded by people who would today be called "the religious right" and its organization was created by conser-vative businessmen. Moreover, what destroyed slavery in the non-Western world was "Western imperialism." Nothing could be more jolting and discordant with the vision of today's intellectuals

than the fact that it was businessmen, devout reli-
gious leaders and Western imperialists who together
destroyed slavery around the world.

William Wilberforce was one of the twelve Christian men who met in London in 1787 to begin fighting for abolition. Christians also led the fight for civil rights. Dr. Martin Luther King, Jr., rightly celebrated along with Washington and Lincoln as one of America's greatest citizens, was a Baptist minister whose message to the American people was saturated in faith. The black church was the backbone of the civil rights movement. People who reject Christianity, who turn their noses up at the religious origins of Christmas, are also rejecting the faith of many of the men and women who have made this world a better place: Martin Luther King, Jr., William Wilberforce, Mother Teresa.

There's a helpful thought experiment to determine whether Bible-believing is really such a bad thing, brought to you by radio host Dennis Prager. He once asked his listeners to shut their eyes and imagine that their car has broken down one night in a not-so-nice neighborhood. A group of young twenty-something men are walking down the street toward the car. He then asked listeners if it would make them feel safer knowing that the young men (a) just got out of a local movie theater after seeing the latest shoot-'em-up action flick, or (b) just got out of their weekly men's Bible study group? The answer is obvious to anyone who is intellectually honest.

Faith is a force of good in this society, and we stigmatize it to our cultural detriment. There's more at stake than we might first think when the public schools start removing "O Come All Ye Faithful" from their choral repertoire—the further deterioration of the principles on which our culture thrives best will soon follow.

Third, Christianity is the source of these ever more illusive "values" we've been talking about. What an arrogant statement, I can almost hear the critics think. You might be an atheist or an agnostic, and you certainly have values. Right? You're a good person.

Well, a friend of mine always says that you can't hear the good news of the Gospel without first hearing the bad news. The bad news is this: You aren't that great. We ain't. Human beings are not inherently good, and—left to our own devices—we tend toward evil. The great Catholic theologian G. K. Chesterton said, "Certain new theologians dispute original sin, which is the only part of Christian theology which can really be proved." The evidence of man's true nature is all around us. Just open the newspaper.

So what's wrong? Well, the Bible diagnoses the human condition in pretty stark terms. Genesis tells the story of the Garden of Eden, where every part of men and women—our minds, emotions, and desires—became corrupted. The book of Romans tells us that we naturally resist God, that all have sinned, and that the result of sin is death. This means we're doomed to spend eternity paying the penalty for our sins.

Well, that certainly qualifies as "bad news," doesn't it?

And this applies to us all. Even "good" people commit sins all the time. We might not be as patient with our kids, we might swipe some supplies from work, we might cheat on our taxes—or, worse, our spouses. And some of us often even do good works for selfish motivations.

Once we realize the bad news, we're certainly ready to hear the good news (which is what the word "gospel" literally means, by the way). You'd think the Gospel really should be good news for everyone, but it's not. Turns out, it's only good news to people who realize they were in a bad situation to start with. If doctors announced a miracle cure, only the people who believed the disease existed would be thrilled. Nonbelievers would meet the announcement with a giant yawn.

This is frequently where liberals and conservatives part ways.

Liberals tend to believe people are good, and institutions like the church or the traditional family are actually oppressive. Get rid of these bad institutions, or fundamentally transform them beyond recognition, and people will thrive and flourish. Ahhh, man-made Utopia.

By contrast, conservatives tend to believe that people aren't that great to start with. And without faith and family to guide us and reinforce values that often go against our selfish desires, we'll drift toward our own destruction.

See why the "culture wars" matter so much? Many on the Left see faith and family as oppressive, but the Right sees them as indispensable. And that's why the fight is so ferocious. And that's why the outcome matters so much.

Doubt this analysis? Consider the difference in the way the two sides govern.

Liberals take the power away from parents to raise their kids, giving even very young teens abortion pills (but forbid Tylenol for a seventeen-year-old student at school, and cancel her field trip to walk to the local library without signed parental consent). They put the power of the state over religious freedom, constantly trying to narrow religious exemptions to laws, forcing people of faith to violate their consciences as the price of doing business, and ever more confining churches to the sphere of private "worship." They even try to change the definition of marriage, to elevate adult desires over the societal cornerstone that's built the family since the beginning of time.

But it gets more nonsensical. Because they believe the enlightened elite are so good by nature—having removed the oppressive power of faith and family—they concentrate power in the hands of the state, handing the keys of our economy, of our businesses, of our homes, and of our churches to officials who, it turns out, are just as prone to abuse and evil as anyone else. Unfortunately, because these leaders have so much power, the abuse and incompetence occur on a grand scale.

But the liberals have it wrong. The truly enlightened realize power can't be concentrated, and the state does not know better than the family and the church. One of the reasons why crony capitalism and so-called big-government conservatism infuriate me so much is that they're simply slightly airbrushed versions of liberalism. Conservatives who buy into the premises of liberalism are not conservatives at all.

Our Founders implemented a system of checks and balances not because people are good but because people can't be trusted with power. And because we're not that great, we need constant reminders of our need for God. As the little kids sing in Sunday school, "they are weak, but He is strong." Remove those reminders, scrub the world of any mention of His presence, and we make it that much harder to do what's right.

You're not being "tolerant" when you censor yourself; you're contributing to our decline.

Mark Levin made this very point in his book *Liberty and Tyranny: A Conservative Manifesto*: "How can it be said, as it often is, that moral order is second to liberty when one cannot survive without the other? A people cannot remain free and civilized without moral purposes, constraints, and duties. What would be left but relativism manifesting itself in anarchy, followed by tyranny and brute force?"

So much of our world can be explained by simply understanding human beings, but not in the hip, self-centered style of pop psychology. God is the only cure for what ails us. C. S. Lewis put it like this: "You and I have need of the strongest spell that can be found to wake us from the evil enchantment of worldliness." That's why the messages your kids get from schools and culture actually matter. We're telling kids like Joey not to cheat on exams, not to do drugs, not to party or sleep around, while stigmatizing the one thing that can empower them to live virtuously: faith in Christ.

That's why the discussion of Christmas is such a big deal.

Are the words of John Adams—that our Constitution was "made only for a moral and religious people"— words of inspiration? Or, because we're so far down this path away from God, are they words that evoke fear?

To answer that question, I need you to go with me on a journey, fifteen years into the future. Grab your coat and mittens, because we're headed to Anchorage.

The year is 2028.

Piper and Santa delivered gifts with me
when I served as head of the state's National
Guard. In 2008 we traveled to various villages
in Alaska to share Christmas joy.

6

Seeing Double . . . Standards

Come in! Come in, and know me better, man!

—SPIRIT OF CHRISTMAS PRESENT IN

A CHRISTMAS CAROL

In *A Christmas Carol*, old Ebenezer is visited during the night by three ghosts: the "Ghost of Christmas Past," the "Ghost of Christmas Present," and the "Ghost of Christmas Yet to Come." Each apparition poses a different vision to old Scrooge. The Ghost of Christmas Yet to Come takes Ebenezer on a trip into the future. And now, I would like to take a similar journey with you . . . minus the ghost part. I never did like those ghosts.

The two visions of Christmas Yet to Come I am about to show you are wildly different. Let's start with the first, which I've dubbed the "Vision of Christmas

Yet to Come . . . if the Militant Atheists and Secular Liberals Have Their Way."

Hold on to your hat.

December 2028, Anchorage, Alaska

"You're early, Nana," Tripp says when he answers the door. I'm always surprised at how tall he is, though I swear he sprouted up yet another foot since starting college.

"Holy. What are they feeding you here?" I ask, tipping my trifocals to peer up at my strapping grandson, the newest recruit on the Seawolves hockey team. He's dressed in team sweats.

"I haven't had moose chili all semester, but the dorm food's decent and Costco's food court is just down the road," he says. "So I'm eating, Nan." Two other big guys show up behind Tripp. He introduces his teammates from Michigan and Minnesota. "We're just about to slap some pucks on the outdoor ice," Tripp says apologetically. "Want me to bag it so we can beat the dinner rush?"

My Christmas dinner with Tripp has become one of my favorite annual traditions. Normally, we meet in Wasilla when everyone comes home for the holidays. However, I had business in Anchorage that day so I decided to surprise him on campus by taking him out early.

"No way," I say. "You play like you practice. So go practice hard. I'll walk you guys to the ice and hang around to see the campus decorations."

As we walk, many people say hello to Tripp, and my heart swells. It seems he's doing really well here, and Bristol is thankful he got that hockey scholarship. I notice all the green and gold Seawolves colors on the students who pass by, but very few Christmas decorations.

We reach one of the outdoor rinks. Tripp leans up against the boards to unload dull practice skates from his bag. "Go stay warm, Nana," Tripp says, "unless you want to be in the net for us? That'll warm you up." I assured him he wouldn't find the net all evening if I were goalie, so I'd let them have their fun. "I'll see you in an hour. Practice so hard that the game'll feel easy."

As I walk back to the ski path toward the student union, I hear him mumble to his Minnesota buddy.

"She's a walking cliché when it comes to motivating me," he says, laughing.

My hearing isn't as good as it used to be, but I heard that. Track always accuses me of being a "walking cliché," with all my little quotes and snippets I throw out during speeches and general conversation. I guess Tripp thought he could use the same phrase to make his friends laugh. "Did you mean to say I was a walking encyclopedia of good advice?"

Tripp asks, "What's an encyclopedia?"

I wave him off, and let the boys discuss what one calls a "relic from the eighties," before the familiar sounds of blade scrapes and slapshots muffle their "olden days" musings. I walk through the student union and grab a cup of coffee.

When I hand the cashier my money, I say, "Merry Christmas," and she looks at me with dull eyes.

I notice there's dullness everywhere. There are no traditional Christmas decorations. Everything holiday-related is brass and silver. There are pinecones and candles arranged beautifully around the student center, but no mention of Christmas at all.

I walk to an electronic message board, and read the neon flashing across a screen.

"As we approach the Winter Solstice season, which encompasses holidays celebrated by many faiths, keep in mind the University of Alaska

Anchorage is a diverse community and diversity is one of our key educational values."

A few advertisements flicker on and off the screen, and I stand mesmerized by this colorful contrast to its gray surroundings. When I was in college, we had thumbtacked bulletin boards, ratty paper advertisements with phone numbers written vertically at the bottom. If you wanted guitar lessons, or a job picking potatoes on the Palouse, or directions to the next kegger, you'd rip off a little slip of paper, stick it in your pocket, and accidentally run it through the washing machine by the time you needed the information. This was a definite upgrade.

So what was going on at Tripp's college this week? A piano concert, a ski trip, a French class in Paris, and a spirituality group meeting. Maybe I should go with Tripp to a meeting of one of his Christian fellowship groups on campus, I think. That's when ads for various UAA lectures catch my eye.

THE CHRISTMAS MYTH: REDISCOVERING THE
PAGAN ROOTS OF A HIJACKED HOLIDAY

FAMILY, FRIENDS, AND LOVE: CELEBRATING
THE HOLIDAYS WITHOUT INVITING
THE GODS OF YESTERYEAR

SHOULD YOU TRUST YOUR PARENTS AGAIN?
RECOVERING FROM THE SANTA LIE

I stifle a groan. I'd rather go vegan for a day than sit through those lectures.

"Excuse me," I say to a person who looks official. She is scurrying by in a business suit, heading into an administration office. "I'm visiting my grandson, and I have a few questions."

She smiles warmly and welcomes me into the office. "You look vaguely familiar, please come in," she says, motioning toward a sitting area. She gives me the once-over. "Hey. Were you the lady in the old sitcom, say about twenty years ago, about some defunct television network on 30 Rock Street?"

"Nope," I reply.

"Hmmm. Well, I swear I've seen you before, but in any case, I'm Karly, the Vice Dean of Respect and Inclusion." She was still searching the recesses of her mind for some irrelevant connection when she asked, "How can I help you?"

"It's nice to meet you, Karly. I'm here because every year I take my grandson out for dinner," I explain, adding, "It's our little Christmas tradition."

Was it my imagination, or did her smile suddenly freeze?

"I was hoping to find some sort of Christmas event here on campus before taking him out to eat," I say. *"You know, to see what his life is like here, now that he's all grown up."*

"Sure," the lady says, reaching for some pamphlets. *"While we don't actually have any 'Christmas' activities per se,"* she says, *"um, this is a very diverse community, I'm sure you'll be able to find something you'll enjoy. There's the Winter Solstice gathering at seven o'clock tonight."*

"What is that, exactly?" I ask. *"Like, caroling?"*

"Well, last year, solstice celebrators had a bonfire, they made a representation of a man out of sticks, and they tucked little pieces of paper into the man's hand with regrets from the last year. Then they lit it on fire and watched it burn away their shame and guilt," she says. *"Then they had sausages, eggs, and lots of good traditional drink."*

"Oh," I say. *"Well, that sounds . . . interesting."*

"Okay, let me see . . . ," she says while thumbing through the information. *"We have a Saturnalia party tonight, but I'm not sure you'd enjoy that loutish scene."* She laughs, and I laugh, too, even

though I don't find this very amusing. As I'd told college students years earlier in one particularly fun and raucous speech, "You guys out there today had better be thinking Sam Adams more than drinking Sam Adams."

"Well, what about Christmas-type events?" I ask, very slowly so perhaps she can understand me. "You know, wise men, an angel, star over Bethlehem? That type of thing?" I pause. "Ring a bell?"

She frowns. "We aren't really into the religious aspects of the holiday," she says. "Since there are so many religions represented here on campus, we try to keep faith as a personal thing for students."

"Sure," I say, "I get it. "This is a diverse campus that values diversity, where everyone should be welcomed and tolerated. I'll just go look at the message board to find where the Christian student groups are meeting and ask them directly."

Karly sighs. "You might have a problem. Most of the Christian organizations have opted not to participate in our inclusive community, so we have no knowledge of their schedules or activities. You'd have to contact them independently, and I can't offer their contact information, but their events would be decidedly off campus."

I don't have much time to spend tracking down non-campus-related ministries because the boys come off the ice in less than an hour. Plus, I just want to see Tripp in his college element, not drag him off campus for some spiritual lesson. "It used to be that Christmas events happened all over the campus."

"Yes, but times change," she says, looking at me with concern or pity. "We don't have slavery anymore, either."

What did Miss Karly just say? I inaudibly gulp. Did this gal just compare me wanting to celebrate Christmas to the evils of slavery? Surely I'm misunderstanding her, I think as I glance down at the pamphlet she handed me. It reads, "UAA—Faith and Spirituality Guide for Campus Life."

"Ma'am, I'm heading across campus," she says. "I'd suggest you try the multi-faith center. Perhaps they'll have what you're looking for. Want me to show you where it is?" She kicks off her Birkenstocks and slips on spiked synthetic mukluks to walk outside.

By this time, curiosity gets the better of me so I follow her out the main door, which is adorned with festive fruits like pomegranates, pineapples, and pears. She sees me poke at the globose fruit to see if it's real, while I'm wondering why they couldn't have at least added a candy cane to add some traditional "diversity" to their door decoration. "They're fake," she answers my unasked question, adding, "Crowns of calyx lobes aren't indigenous to Alaska." No kidding, Sherlock, I want to respond, but bite my tongue and keep walking.

We pass a parking lot of Christmas trees, with students holding signs printed $10.

"That sure beats having to cut down your own Christmas tree," I say to the vice dean. She points to the signage above the parking lot. "Yes, all proceeds go to sustainable rain forests," she explains. "There's no other way to really justify killing so many trees, right?"

I look at the sale, and see a gigantic banner printed in black:

HOLIDAY TREE SALE

As if reading my mind, Karly says, "We use inclusive language all across the campus."

Yippy skippy, I'm tempted to retort. But again I bite my tongue and move on. Out of the corner of my eye, I see a little shack set up across the quad, with a warm glowing light coming out of it.

"Look at that," I say, wondering how a Nativity scene made its way onto campus.

"Oh, that's our 'natural nativity,'" she says proudly. "It's recognizing the rebirth of the Unconquered Sun."

Sure enough, as we trudge through the snow and get closer to the display, I realize it's no Nativity scene at all. I notice there's a girl doll nestled in the hay.

"Who's that?" I ask.

"Do we really want to teach our female students to sit around waiting for a male savior?" she asks conspiratorially. I figure she believes since we are both female, we must at least agree on her anti-male sentiment. Instead of an angel, an astronaut hovers above the manger. "This represents what kind of scientific advancement we can achieve when not encumbered by religious superstition. Also, check out the wise men." Three mannequins stand by the manger, dressed as Albert Einstein, Thomas Edison, and Charles Darwin. A sign next to the scene reads:

THOU SHALL NOT STEAL

"Scripture?" I ask, incredulously. "Is that university-approved?"

"It's kind of a fun allusion to the fact that Christmas was stolen from the pagans."

"But of course," I mumble. I've begun to lose my appetite.

I know it was eons ago when I was a student, but when did things get so bad? I found it interesting that Christian groups that weren't deemed "inclusive" are forbidden to be on campus. What did that even mean? The school sanctions events to worship the "sun god," but it won't stomach groups that worship the real God? Ironically, with Anchorage's dark winter days, the sun barely peeks over the horizon before dipping right back down again. At least theirs would be a quick worship, I figure. The public-funded university also promotes agendas that blatantly mock traditional Christmas displays, I realize as I make a mental file of other examples I've just seen. It's hard for me to sort through this during our trek in fresh powder, as Karly continues to yammer away. As we trudge forward, suddenly a scene in the university's park stops me dead in my tracks.

"Is that a . . . crucifixion scene?" I gasp.

"Why, yes, it is," Karly says. "One of our clubs put that up to make a statement against the 'religious' aspects of the holiday season."

I look more closely. There, on the wooden cross, a plastic skeleton hangs, wearing a red Santa Claus hat.

"I think their message is to finally put an end to the Christian myth," *she explains further.*

With that, I decide not to ask my young tour guide any more questions about religion. I obviously understand college is a place to expand your mind, to grow, to challenge preconceived ideas. However, who is challenging the students' liberal ideas, if all the Christians and conservatives have been marginalized?

"If you need to use the restroom," *Karly helpfully points out,* "we have a brand-new, state-of-the-art facility."

She motions toward a gleaming building that I can tell is very near completion. "What kind of bathroom is 'state-of-the-art'?" *I ask, not even trying to hide my annoyance anymore. Dang, I think, no wonder tuition is so high if they brag about their toilets.*

That's when I see the welded metal sign hanging above the door:

RESTROOM AND FOOT-WASHING STATION

Then I notice a combined "female" *and* "male" *symbol above their gender-neutral bathroom doors.*

"Our Muslim students partake in wudu, the ritual ablutions before the prayer sessions. They had a hard time washing their feet in the sinks, so adding foot-washing stations was part of our university renovations. Costly in terms of budget, sure, but here we believe inclusion is, well, priceless."

I duck my head into the "state-of-the-art" commode and sure enough, along the wall, in the corner, are several "foot baths."

"How many students use this 'priceless' spigot?" Eh . . . I realize before I can stop myself how futile my inquiry is. As anticipated, Karly just looks at me like, "What difference does it make at this point?"

I could use that 1981 Christmas dictionary from my parents right about now, because no words can express the way I am feeling at this moment.

Just a couple of buildings away from the not-so-jolly crucified St. Nick and the foot soaks stands a beautiful multi-faith center. The vice dean pushes open another citrus-adorned door and shakes snow-flakes off her coat. It's warm and cozy in here, there's some kind of artificial fire glowing in a central glass fireplace, and I'm assuming it's fueled by natural gas as it radiates exactly what our bodies shiver for. I look up to see students taking down a sign, which reads:

ANCHORAGE HONORS EID AL-ADHA

"Eid is the Muslim holiday about spending time with family and friends, sacrifice, and thanksgiving." The vice dean smiles and says, "Since both Thanksgiving and Eid celebrate family and sharing, it's the perfect example of co-religion cooperation that's embraced here."

"Kumbaya," I say. I wonder if local Eid observers have any luck tracking down a camel for their Festival of Sacrifice. I saw a caribou the other day, but not since my Middle East trips to visit our troops as head of the Alaska National Guard had I crossed a camel's path.

"I appreciate your help, Karly," I tell her sincerely. I have learned a lot on our walk. I continue to scan her literature. The pamphlet in my hand purports to evaluate each faith and religion for its acceptability, for its embrace of diversity. Right there, in black and white, is the comparison of traditional biblical ideas about morality next to writings on how the Bible can be used to justify slavery. Those who hold traditional views are explicitly compared to "slave owners."

The way Bristol has raised Tripp—and the way I was raised and in turn raised her—is marked in the brochure under a drawing of a traffic light with the red light illuminated. As in, "stop—do not go" to these types of services. By this time, I'm seeing red, even though there isn't even a glimmer of Christmas decor anywhere.

"I must be confused," I say, holding up the pamphlet. "Silly me, but what Christian groups are represented in this so-called multi-faith center?"

"Well, all faiths are represented," she says proudly. "Islam, Hinduism, paganism, Christianity . . ."

"What type of Christianity?" I interrupt.

"Well, as I mentioned, some of the Christian groups do not want to be a part of our inclusive campus."

"So"—I don't wait for her to explain the obvious—"you exclude them from your inclusive campus?"

"Well," she says, looking a little shocked, "they really exclude themselves by their bigotry. If you consult chart three in your pamphlet," she says, opening it up, "we itemize some of the reasons why they aren't here."

"Oh, I see." I look at the tiny print. "UAA believes traditional Christian theology is sexist, patriarchal, racist, and"—a nice touch—"homophobic."

"There's much more than that," she says, smiling. "But we had to limit to a few phrases to get it into our pocket-sized chart."

"But you built foot-washing stations for one group?" I ask.

"At this institution for higher learning we embrace diversity and affirmatively reject Islamophobia," she says, tweaking her head and clenching her teeth but never losing her labored smile. Just then, Tripp and his buddies come through the door. That omnipresent, distinct hockey smell precedes them.

"Nana?" Tripp says, interrupting what was becoming a pretty terse conversation. "Where'd you go? You disappeared like a willow ptarmigan."

"You said you were going to skate," I say.

"Yeah, we had to leave," he explains. "There was a sign that said men were banned from the facilities until later tonight."

The vice dean jumps in to clarify. "UAA is trying to accommodate Muslim women who don't feel comfortable exercising in front of men."

"Karly, you'll correct me if I'm wrong, but aren't the Muslim organizations more restrictive regarding gender roles and sexuality than these other groups, like the Christians? Aren't homosexuals regularly put to death in Muslim countries?"

"I'm growing concerned about this line of questioning," she says. "Our Islamic students come from a rich cultural heritage . . . one that's been

*oppressed and forgotten in the West. It's important
they feel welcomed and honored here."*

*"What about just your average Joe Six-Pack
boring ol' Christian student feeling welcomed and
honored?"*

*"Oh, please," she says. "The dominant faith in
our culture doesn't need more of an advantage than
it already enjoys."*

This version of Christmas Yet to Come doesn't sound
very merry, does it?

Though society has yet to resemble the story above,
we're edging ever closer to that kind of reality. But it
doesn't have to be this way. Something amazing can
happen when people refuse to let the police of political correctness ruin our federal holiday (. . . or our
universities).

I invite you on another trip with me. Instead of going
into the future we're careening toward at an alarming
rate, let's journey into an America of true religious
freedom and tolerance.

December 2028, Anchorage, Alaska

*"Let's go through the quad and grab a bite to
eat," Tripp says, greeting me as he opens the door
and gives me a bear hug.*

"You're just happy to get free food," I choke out from under his embrace. I take a step back and look up at my oldest grandchild. "What do you want to eat?"

"Just something on campus. It'll be faster."

"You sure, Triple Threat?" I refer to him by the newborn nickname we gave him eighteen years ago. He arrived during an intense NBA season, which managed to add constant "white noise" in our living room where he spent most waking hours. In basketball, the best, most threatening competitors master the three fundamentals of basketball. So we called Tripp "Triple Threat" for his masterful infant trifecta grasp of sleeping, eating, and regurgitating.

As we head down to find food, he tells me all about his hockey schedule, but stops short when we see a group of carolers in his dorm's lobby.

"We wish you a Merry Christmas," they sing. "We wish you a Merry Christmas . . ."

We skirt around the singers and head to the doors. But before we slip out to the dark campus grounds, I stop and join in on the song. "Good tidings we bring . . ."

Tripp, never a fan of my singing, grabs my arm and pulls me out of the lobby.

"Seriously, Nana," he says. "I'm starving."

The snow on the sidewalks crunches underfoot.

"So, are you getting any studying done between practices?" I ask. He just grins.

I know he wants to change the subject back to the ice, and I don't press. Since I'm Grandma, I can indulge him and leave it to his mother to nag about grades.

"Will your jersey sport the C this season, honey?" I know his big dream is to become captain of the team.

"I doubt I'll be named captain, Nana," he answers. I see his shoulders pull back taller and stronger while explaining. "But that's okay, because our team's strong, and the upperclassmen deserve to lead."

"Awesome, Tripp." I'm pleased to hear his answer. "'Remember there's no limit to what a man can do if he doesn't mind who gets the credit.' So said Ronald Reagan."

"Thank you, Walking Cliché," he says. I was going to lecture him about the definition of "cliché" when we walk by a display that makes me gasp.

"What the heck is that?" I ask. There is a crucified plastic skeleton wearing nothing but a Santa Claus hat, nailed to a cross.

We get closer and see two young men manning two booths. One is the "natural nativity" and the other is the "Santa Crucifixion." There are two other students standing nearby and they're engaged in impassioned conversation, so we walk slowly to figure out what's going on. One girl is talking.

"So," I hear her say to the guy next to the display, "you laugh and mock, you thump your chest proclaiming atheism, but you asked so I answered: That's why we believe this whole 'manger' and 'ass' story. Now, are you sorry you asked?"

"If you're interested," says her bundled-up friend with a smile, "you can read more about it in this."

"Gee, thanks," one of the guys says as he reluctantly reaches to take the offered pamphlet from her boxing-glove-sized mittens with his own clumsily covered extremities.

"I'll read it," he says, begrudgingly. "But only if you come to our 'Separate the Myth from the Holiday' conference next week."

"Actually," the atheist's partner on his left says, "since you guys like to talk so much, you should come and represent the other point of view. If you have the stomach for it."

"It would take more than you guys to intimidate us," they say with a laugh. "Count us in."

I watch them walk across the sidewalk where they've set up the one, competing Nativity scene. Their display glows with warm light illuminating the baby wrapped in swaddling clothes tucked in a hay-filled crate. We hear "Away in the Manger" softly emanating from some tiny speakers hidden in the dry grass. Next to their scene, they have a sign that says:

CELEBRATE CHRISTMAS WITH THE UAA
FELLOWSHIP OF CHRISTIAN ATHLETES

"Where should we eat, Tripp?" I wave at the girls who are now busy substituting handshakes with goose-down-fattened fist-pumps with friends passing by. It's fun to see people advocating for their beliefs so passionately, especially with humor and humility.

"Anywhere," he says. "Actually, I need Mom to put more credits on my meal account."

"Get a job, big guy," I reply. He knew I was going to say that.

Just then, we walk upon the digital kiosk flashing the news of the day across a screen. The student host appears at the top of the screen, and I marvel at how much more effective these kiosks are than the bulletin boards when I was in school. "In national news, President-elect Romney is preparing to finally move into the White House."

"I guess the sixth time's the charm," I say. The host is explaining the transition to the new administration, while photos flash across the screen.

"I must find out the secret to his fabulous hair," I mutter. "How can it still look that good?"

"Maybe he doesn't use that seven-dollar root touch-up in a box," Tripp says, staring down at my scalp.

"Hey, that's only when I can't bribe Willow to do it," I say, mesmerized by the screen. "And look at him posing with all the students of that enormous school. His hair hasn't faded one bit over the years."

"That's not Mitt visiting a school," Tripp corrects me. "That's the Romney family Christmas card."

A student sees us reading the notices about upcoming speeches and elbows into our space. "You should come hear an amazing lecture tonight," he says. "It's superb. It's called, 'Should You Trust Your Parents Again? Recovering from the Santa Lie.'"

"Thanks, man. I'll be there," Tripp says, smiling at me.

I give him the evil eye and say, "I'll make sure Santa knows you've outgrown him."

"I don't care if Santa knows," he said. "Just don't tell Mom."

The kiosk advertises many goings on around campus that month: Pancha Ganapati for Hindus, Hanukkah for Jews, a coalition of different Christian denominations getting together to serve the poor in Anchorage.

"Look," I point to the screen. "That one's going on now." Sure enough, as we walked to the student food court, we see students sitting around a roaring bonfire. They're singing as we approach, but a kid gets up to speak and quiets the group to thank everyone for showing up.

"Today, we're going to participate in Anchorage's Annual Community Christmas Feast! You ready to serve?"

"Hey, Tripp!" one of the guys at the back of the crowd yells, as the students move in to grab aprons. "You coming?"

Tripp looks at me and smiles. "Well, you always say you want to do something different for dinner."

We both snag Rudolph-inspired red aprons and try to fit them over our puffy coats as we head down *to the community center, where Tripp hands out food to people in need.*

I've never been prouder.

These are two very different visions of the future. And we have the power to create one or the other. There is so much at stake.

Let's look at that first vision I painted above. Yes, the one I titled the rather unimaginative "Vision of Christmas Yet to Come . . . if the Militant Atheists and Secular Liberals Have Their Way." (Hey, I'm not Charles Dickens.) Well, I didn't just make up those almost unbelievable examples. Everything in that section (except our Triple Threat growing up in the blink of an eye, obviously) is based on true-life events that have *already happened* in America. They didn't all happen at once on the same campus, but they happened, and they will happen more frequently the more we sit idly by without taking a stand against this political correctness run amok.

Doubt it? Here are the real-life counterparts of the examples embedded in that vision:

FOOT-WASHING STATIONS: In 2007, at the University of Michigan–Dearborn, university officials installed $25,000 foot-washing stations in campus restrooms after having talks with the Muslim Students'

Association about better accommodating their daily rituals.

WOMEN-ONLY GYM HOURS: In 2008, Harvard announced women-only gym hours to accommodate Muslim women who did not feel comfortable exercising in the presence of males.

But what is the real issue here? In a word (à la Joe Biden): "double standard." We all appreciate religious liberty, but it should be liberty *for all,* not favoritism for some. Sadly, that's the way it's playing out on American campuses. For example, a college will not grant any accommodation to Christian students requesting exemptions from nondiscrimination policies to allow them to select Christian leaders for their groups, but it will actively discriminate on the basis of gender to create "female-only" gym or pool hours for people of other faiths. The foot baths are examples of colleges spending tens of thousands of dollars to make select students feel more welcome, even as they spend hundreds of thousands of dollars in legal fees to defund traditional Christian groups and toss them from campus. Universities are sending an unambiguous message: We will bend and break our own nondiscrimination rules, while spending a great deal of your money to accommodate other faiths. Yet we will bend or break constitutional law, while also spending a lot of your money to toss Christian groups off campus.

It's a ridiculous double standard.

NATURAL NATIVITY SCENE: In 2011, the Freedom from Religion folks put up their "natural nativity" at the Wisconsin Capitol. Instead of recognizing the birth of Christ, like most nativities, theirs purports to recognize the "rebirth of the Unconquered Sun"; has floating astronauts instead of angels; honors Darwin, Einstein, and Edison instead of the biblical Magi; and has a THOU SHALT NOT STEAL sign to shame Christians for celebrating Christmas as a religious holiday.

SANTA CRUCIFIXION: In 2011, an atheist organization put up a "crucified" Santa outside the courthouse in Leesburg, Virginia, to the horror of many of the town's children. These crucifixions have since popped up in several towns across the nation.

CHRISTIAN GROUPS BEING KICKED OFF CAMPUS FOR NOT BEING "INCLUSIVE" ENOUGH: Vanderbilt University— located in the "buckle of the Bible belt"—made Christian groups sign contracts that said they'd be open to having atheist and actively homosexual leadership. The Catholic and evangelical Christian groups refused to sign the contracts—except one that chickened out and signed—leaving hundreds of Vanderbilt students without spiritual leadership on campus. Sadly, Vanderbilt is only one of dozens of colleges that have tried a similar tactic.

UNIVERSITIES EVALUATING VARIOUS RELIGIONS: Georgia Institute of Technology created an ironically titled "Safe Space" training manual for students, which helpfully compared Christians to slave owners:

> *Many religious traditions have taught, and some continue to teach, that homosexuality is immoral. These condemnations are based primarily on a few isolated passages from the Bible. Historically, biblical passages taken out of context have been used to justify such things as slavery, the inferior status of women, and the persecution of religious minorities.*

A similar publication at the University of Michigan mocked Bible believers in this way:

> *Some texts of the Old Testament are used to condemn homosexuality. Taken literally and out of context, biblical passages can be used to justify slavery, prohibit the wearing of red dresses and*

eating of shrimp and shellfish, and to reinforce the inferiority of women.

Here's the bottom line.

Our government has already taken it upon itself to teach your college students how to interpret the Bible. Were you led to believe radical liberals were all about "separation of church and state"? Hardly. They'll stuff their theology down your kids' collective throats before you've had a chance to unload their dorm gear from your trunk.

Perhaps the "Ghost of Christmas Present" costume fits me just fine, because the dystopia I presented at the beginning of the chapter is already happening all over America.

Yet all is not lost. In the Dickens classic, after Ebenezer saw the present and the future, he knew he had to do something. So, instead of retreating, he determined to make changes in his heart and in his community.

We can, too.

With special, child-like faith...

In 2008, supercute Trig starred on the state of
Alaska governor's Christmas cards.

7

Who'd Make Up a Story Like That?

The only things we can keep are the things we freely give to God. What we try to keep for ourselves is just what we are sure to lose.

—C. S. LEWIS, *MERE CHRISTIANITY*

There's something about stockings all lined up in a row, each one holding surprises for the fortunate owner whose name is embroidered in green or red on the front. Stockings represent a simpler time, when Christmas gifts didn't require chargers, and kids were more likely to get candy canes than a plastic iTunes gift card. At our house, we don't hang stockings the typical way. We have an enormous mantel—an Alaska original, embedded with fossils we collected by going "fossil hunting" up in the hills—way up in the hills. The mantel would provide a picture-perfect place to hang the stockings, but too many little hands have reached up to sneak a peak too early, only to have stocking hangers land on their heads with a thump (and who wants to spend a perfectly good day under an ice pack?).

Instead, I drape our stockings from the upstairs railing of our stairs, far from the reach of excited children but close enough to admire with anticipation. While Track was getting ready for his winter Afghanistan deployment, I finally put away his twenty-two-year-old stocking I'd purchased at a crafts fair in Eagle River as a new mom with two toddlers.

We were the goofy new parents who assumed our favorite sport would be the kids' favorite, too, as if they'd inherited a passion for the hardwood in their DNA. The cute and clever stocking had gotten thinner over the years, but it still had the cartoon bear wearing a green-and-gold University of Alaska basketball jersey. The smiling bear was holding up a basketball, and I remember Todd and me both encouraging our firstborn, Track, to pick up the sport—our favorite sport—when he was little.

"Want to shoot hoops?" I'd ask. "Just like the little bear on your stocking?"

He did eventually play, and even played on various basketball teams.

All the kids did end up playing basketball, and Track even took up our shared point guard position, but— year after year—I could tell he wasn't obsessed with it. Darn it! Every Christmas when I unpacked his stocking I realized he was growing further away from his naïve parents' dream of him playing this less physical, warmer indoor sport. Finally, in high school, he left the hardwood for full-time ice time, and even moved to Michigan as an exchange player for a year of upper-level competitive hockey.

"What were you thinking, Mom?" Track asked me one Christmas as he held up that stocking and pointed to the James Naismith–honoring bear. "I couldn't stick with a sport where the whistle blows every time you bump someone."

Spoken like a true hockey player.

When I finally decided to replace his old basketball bear stocking, I ran my fingers over the stitching that spelled his name. I know it's different, but I love the name Track. And I love my boy more than life itself. An unexpected big fat lump formed in my throat while I decided what to do with that old stocking I bought as a harried young mom. *How could his childhood already be over?* I wondered. How could the same little boy who hoped so desperately for indoor Nerf nets and pucks in his stocking suddenly be packing his things for another military deployment?

I forced the thought from my head, as I found Bristol's stocking, which also had that smiling teddy bear on the front, only hers was wearing a frilly pink tutu and figure skates.

If I had been less than prophetic in choosing the UAA basketball motif for Track, then I'd have to say I nailed Bristol's! It just took a while. Of course, she was an outdoorsy, athletic, studious kid. So much so that once, after her big brother trash-talked her self-proclaimed "toughness," she joined the youth league football team. Really, her nonglamorous life in Alaska was so far removed from a ballerina dancer's that I figured I got her stocking choice wrong, too. Until, when she was nineteen, she fulfilled her Christmas teddy bear's frilly pink tutu destiny when she got a call from the TV show *Dancing with the Stars* and loaded up her truck and moved to Beverly—Hills, that is. Movie stars and Bristol, who'd never danced a step in her life. (As she corrected Jay Leno on a *Tonight Show* appearance wherein Jay assumed she had at least gotten to dance at her high school prom. "No, Jay, I didn't even dance at my prom," she said. "I was pregnant, remember?") Bristol danced her way into the finals of the show! Two years later she cha-cha-cha'd her way to the All-Star season and taught us all a great life lesson along the way. Bristol, always cognizant of the harsh critics and their rants against her participation, declared to me, "Heh! Exactly! The critics are going to criticize anyway, and the haters are going to hate, *so you might as well dance!*" And she went on to buy herself a home with her winnings.

Yep, in all things, you might as well dance!

I put the big kids' stockings aside. The rest of the crew would forge their own paths independent of any stocking bears' wishes. The next three kids had to settle for those cheapo red furry stockings from the grocery store that were personalized only when they wrote their names in glitter across the white fake-fur trim.

Last year, I finally decided it was time to make new stockings. I bought felt and collected fur from old pelts we had around the house. And then for an extra-nice touch, I had a bit of help from my dad, his buddy Adrian Lane, and my dad's most loyal, low-maintenance friend, his dog Bo.

Bo is a trained antler hunter. The agile, crackerjack lab finds antlers that have been shed in the woods and hidden around mounds of camouflaged tundra and tenaciously retrieves them. (Dad, forever the science teacher, collects everything under the sun to more easily teach natural science to the layman. In his house, he practically has a museum, but his antler pile is perhaps the most notable feature. Towering twelve feet high in the yard, it is the grandest Christmas tree in all Wasilla when he strings lights around it in December. You may have seen it on Larry the Cable Guy's hilarious show.) Dad and Adrian would sit watching *Monday Night Football*, sawing, sanding, and carving buttons for my stockings out of various species' antlers—including the Monsterous Cardestroyerous and Rangifer Tarandus. (See, Dad? I learned something from your natural science lessons! Or maybe I just googled it to honor you and Bo. But that counts for something, right?)

When I sewed the buttons to the brown felt, it gave the stockings a wild frontier flair, along with Chuck Heath's lovingly rugged touch.

You won't find that on Pinterest.

Which—honestly—might be a good thing. Sometimes seeing photos of all the impossibly perfect Christmas crafts, family activities, multi-course meals, or spiritual disciplines might make your own season feel . . . well, kind of weak. A quick glance at the grocery checkout line's holiday magazine covers is enough to humble us and admit we'd never pull off the perfect Christmas dinner table, even if we follow the promised "ten easy tips." Just looking at friends' photos of their homemade three-tier cakes, their calm, nonchaotic cookie exchange parties, and their perfectly coiffed children wearing pajamas-that-fit (and even match) is enough to create a feeling of total inadequacy. (Even reading books like this might make you feel like your own season didn't have enough snow.) It makes me appreciate Willow's insistence, though, that plain ol' Rice Krispies treats are all anyone *really* wants at Christmastime.

Deep down, we all sometimes feel Christmas just sometimes fails. We don't quite pull it off. We buy obligatory gifts people don't need and are disappointed when they aren't over-the-crest-of-the-new-fallen-snow thrilled to receive them. We sometimes spend too much, making our January budget uncomfortably stressed. Families annoy us with unrealistic requests; hypersensitive nerves too easily fray amid busy schedules and too many demands on limited time. Pounds of sweets on the lips go right to the hips and workout routines get chucked up the chimney. Plus, there are too many pictures, or too few. Too much eggnog . . . or not enough. Sometimes the day, or the whole doggone season, doesn't live up to our Magi-level expectations.

And here's a confession. Palin family Christmases aren't always characterized by caribou button stockings, blueberry pie pleasures, moose posing in the driveway, and not even a drop of cocoa spilled by the fire (though the moose are pretty much always a given). What I've found over the years is that life doesn't stop for Santa's sleigh.

A few years ago, for example, I'd prepared for a festive Christmas. I made sure to get off the speaking circuit early so I could go crazy with the decorations—just like Piper likes it—and could take my time to thoughtfully choose presents for loved ones. After Todd, Bristol, and I wrapped up a Haitian mission trip with Samaritan's Purse, I made a long to-do list on that long red-eye back to Alaska. Thankfully, the jet lag was minimal, so I was actually able to get home and check off some Christmas-related tasks. I was able to pull off our traditional preparations—with extra baking—rather successfully. At the end of the day, I felt satisfyingly exhausted. The cookies were cooling, the presents were wrapped, and all was well.

On Christmas Eve, everyone gathered at Mom and Dad's. The dog was there, but they were not. After some time of just making ourselves at home and patiently imploring the youngest cousins to be patient, the phone rang.

"Oh, God, no," my sister said to the caller after she listened for just a few moments. That got our attention.

"What is it?" I asked, but she waved me off so she could hear what was being said. Dread filled me as I waited for her to get off the phone. Her tone sent a chill through me that was unrelated to the snowdrifts outside.

"We'll be right there," she said before hanging up the phone and looking at us all. Then she said something that chilled us.

"Dad."

Whoever was on the other end of the phone line gave us precious little information, but we got enough to be alarmed. Dad was rushed to the hospital, Mom was at his bedside. Please hurry. The Heath living room was always full of ivory carvings, mastodon tusks, old Japanese glass fishing floats found while beachcombing, pieces of petrified wood, and other Alaska artifacts. But at that moment, it was full of people in complete shock. We stood in silence, speculating about how dire Dad's situation was. Would he make it until Christmas? I wondered. Scary speculation spread like a Santa Ana wildfire, then Todd opened his mouth and said, "Let's go."

Those two words were enough to jolt the visitors out of their shock and get them scurrying toward the coatrack. People grabbed the nearest jacket, regardless of ownership, slipped on boots, and piled into whatever truck or car was warm enough to start in the dark driveway. We sped convoy-style to Mat-Su Regional Hospital. Molly rode with me in Todd's big Dodge, barreling through the unplowed snow that hid dangerous black ice on Parks Highway.

"This can't be happening," Molly said.

"Dad's always been as healthy as a horse," I said.

"But who really knows with them," Todd asked. "It's not like they tell us what ails them. They never complain about health issues."

"Or about anything else for that matter," I said.

"Dad always says he has the 'skipping heart of an old goat.'" Molly paused as if thinking about that phrase for the first time. "What does that even *mean*?"

"He always said it was no big deal," Todd said. "I know he's on some kind of meds for his heart, because he had it on him when we were out fishing. He laughed me off when I asked him about it. Said it warded off the heebee-jeebies or something."

"I saw him taking those same pills," Molly realized. "But when he washed them down, he said, 'That'll put hair on your chest.'"

"He just takes those to keep his doctor and Mom off his back about eating fewer tons of bacon and more greens," I said. "Not to mention how they nag him about being more careful out on his trapline or at the fishing hole by himself."

Dad always laughed off those concerns with a zestful, "When it's time to go, it's time to go! In the meantime, live life vibrantly! And eat more bacon!" Dad was invincible, we wanted to believe. But the more we compared notes about some aches and pains we'd noticed he suffered, the more we had to come to terms with what was going on.

When we got to the hospital, we met up with the rest of the convoy, poured coffee, and compared notes. I had served for six years on our local hospital's Association Board, but a hospital looks different in the emergency waiting room than it looks in the boardroom.

"Sounds like the sore chest he joked about wasn't really because he flew off, facefirst, from the ladder when he reached too high to fill his bird feeders with his homemade suet recipe last week," I pondered.

And maybe his numb left arm that morning wasn't because he'd fallen asleep on it during an unusually boring ball game he watched with Adrian and their other buddy, Ray.

Todd had walked in the house to make an early delivery of smoked salmon and halibut hors d'oeuvres for that night's party, and stopped to chuckle at the three hard-of-hearing friends zonked out in recliners snoring louder than the game blasting in the background at 8 a.m. Dad looked terribly uncomfortable with his arm and head dangling straight down in front of the chair, Todd said, but he dared not startle him by repositioning his arm, on account of the fact it was dark inside and all three men could be packing.

"And have you noticed," my sister offered, "that he was limping lately?"

"Yeah," I said, "but he told me he hurt it boiling a bear skull."

"What?!" everyone said at once.

It was hard for Dad to shock us anymore, but there in the hospital waiting room we were putting him under extra scrutiny.

"He was sterilizing a skull over a campfire so he could show students how to figure a bear's age based on the condition of its teeth," I said. "The bucket of boiling water spilled over on Dad's foot, but he lunged forward instead of backward because he was more concerned about saving the skull than his foot."

"That sounds like a complete load of bull," Todd said.

"No," Molly said slowly. "I think he was telling the truth on that one, because he told me—and I quote—he 'hurt his hoof while cooking a bear over a campfire.' What does that even mean?" she said. "Normal people stick to s'mores."

"I believe that one, too," I said. "Who'd make up a story like that? Plus, I saw the pictures."

We stopped talking and let this information sink in, as the extended family began showing up in the lobby. We sat silently, then we prayed. Then we listened as my niece offered a prayer no one else wanted to utter.

"Please, God, don't let this be Grandpa's last Christmas," she sweetly asked.

My throat tightened as I wondered if he'd make it to see the next day. "Lord, not on Christmas Eve," I whispered. Todd put his arm around me. "Not on Christmas Eve."

We still hadn't seen Mom, and no one we ran into had any authority to share information with us.

"Why hasn't Mom left his bedside to gather us in?" I asked Todd. I hoped it wasn't because the situation had worsened. In the corner of the waiting room, I saw Bristol talking to her teenage friend, who was a candy-striper for a high school career tech assignment. I wasn't close enough to overhear what her friend was telling Bristol, but I definitely noticed when they sadly embraced. I sure hoped she wasn't violating any HIPAA laws by offering consolation before any of us had to make some major decisions regarding Dad's condition. Bristol's chin was quivering as she began to walk toward us after the conversation.

Just then the doctor walked in the room and said in a calm voice, "You can go on back, guys."

"All of us?" I asked. This wasn't a good sign. There were little kids in the waiting room with us, and I figured they wouldn't let them back unless Dad's situation was really dire.

"Yes," he said, and I swallowed hard as I gathered up the kids and meandered through the hallways behind the doctor to Dad's room. My mind was racing. What should I say to the man who taught me how to fill my freezer with healthy fish and game, to shoot a baseline jumper, to use unforgettable acronyms to memorize planetary alignments, periodic tables, and the preamble to the Constitution, and to find God in the great outdoors? What words could adequately convey my love—my adoration—for probably the most unique father in America?

When the doctor motioned to Dad's room, he said, "It's a good thing you brought him in. Just keep the volume down, okay?"

What a strange request, I thought. Perhaps years of dealing with life-and-death cases had dulled his sensitivity toward grieving family. "And your dad may not be in the bed, so don't be alarmed."

"What are you trying to say?" Todd asked, very directly. The rest of the crew was still too shocked to respond.

"Chances are, he'll be spending a lot of time in the bathroom tonight," the doctor said. "He gave us quite a scare, but we're rehydrating him now."

"You mean . . . ," I prompted him for more information.

"His was one bad case of food poisoning, but it'll pass pretty quickly."

He swung the door open and I looked at Dad, who had a sheepish expression on his face.

"What are you all doing here?" he said with a grin.

In unison, we all called out our names for him: "Dad!" some said. "Grandpa!" came from the children. "Chuck!" from others.

"What did you eat?" I asked, barely able to stop myself from strangling him.

"Salmon," he said.

"That shouldn't kill you," I said, quickly trying to wrap my head around this. "You eat salmon all the time."

" . . . from a can," he added.

"Still," Molly said, biting her lip, "that's not unusual."

My mom, in her kind tone, looked at Dad while clearing her throat, and wondered if he'd volunteer any more information. "Chuck? Honey?"

She tilted her head at her spendthrift husband of fifty years and let us in on a very pertinent detail. "Your father devoured a can of smoked salmon"—she leaned in toward all of us—"that was date-stamped 1992."

"Dad!" the unison yell rang out again. "Grandpa!"

"You ate fish you'd canned while watching Johnny Carson?" I asked with a strange combination of exasperation and elation. "And were surprised that the grim reaper came knocking on your door?"

"Didn't want it to go to waste," Dad said.

He recovered, but we almost killed him.

Mom had just assumed everyone was having a good ol' time under their tree while she sat in the peacefulness of a quiet hospital room listening to carols flow through the intercom while Dad made trips back and forth to the bathroom. She hadn't wanted to bother anyone so didn't call. She figured she'd make it home in time to attend the midnight candlelight service with us.

"Bristol?" I said to my daughter across the room. "What did that candy-striper say to you before you guys hugged out there?"

Apparently, her little HIPAA-respecting friend had just shared some heart-wrenching story of teen angst. I shot darts in her direction while she shrugged her shoulders and said, "But he unfriended her, Mom! Without even texting first!"

It was Dad's antics that gave Christmas a bit of unwanted extra excitement.

But even when everyone was healthy, Christmas wasn't perfect. Todd worked hundreds of miles away up in the North Slope oil fields during the kids' growing-up years. That meant he had a good resource development job, but missed many Christmas mornings while working a "slope schedule" in Prudhoe Bay. He was a production operator near the top of the world, a week on, then a week off. Since there was nothing families could do about a schedule that took the operators away from home half the year, and we were so grateful for a good job he loved—we made the best of it. I convinced the kids early on that there was an upside to Dad missing Christmas.

"We'll always celebrate it twice!"

Most Slope families we knew did the same thing. Our friends kept the tree up and watered until their mom or dad came home, and counted on Santa making a return trip a week or two after December 25. He never failed to deliver.

He didn't deliver much way up there above the Arctic Circle where all the oil is, though. I used to feel sorry for Todd at work on Christmas morning when the corporate culture was, as it should be, to just keep the oil and gas pumping, separated, and flowing down the Trans-Alaska Pipeline. I love it that this fuels our nation with American-made energy sources, and Todd assured me he and his coworkers were all fine with making the best of Christmas in faraway oil field camps. The cafeteria made the day special with extra servings of good meat for the guys. Plus, my husband knew he had lots of little warm, wiggly arms waiting to welcome Daddy home every other Thursday. Not to mention, his wife was equally anxious for the boss to walk through the door. Christmas or not, every other Thursday was always a very good day!

Even when everyone is well and settled in at home, things can get spun up unexpectedly. We Heaths had a tradition that continued when Todd and I started our own family. Every Christmas we get the newest editions of *Ripley's Believe It or Not!* and *Guinness Book of World Records.* Dad's science classroom housed years of the iconic books, and we'd thumb through them at nearly every visit. We'd hover over them and read of the crazy and amazing things people accomplished that year. Accounts of new world records are amusing and sometimes shocking. The daring—or just plain weird—feats kept the kids' interest. As a mom, I loved to hear our kids' funny ideas as they'd wonder aloud about what it would take to set a bizarre or random record. A few years ago, however, one of the girls sat down with our crisp new world records book she'd unwrapped excitedly. I heard her squeal all the way in the kitchen, then start cracking up as she called her sisters to come look.

I glanced over at them at the table, as all of their expressions turned goofy. "What is it?" I asked. Sometimes the records are downright gross, like the world's longest fingernails, or most nails swallowed in one sitting, or most insects living on a willing *Homo sapiens*. "I don't want you guys to have nightmares."

The girls slammed the book shut and giggled.

"Oh, my gosh, Mom!" Willow screamed again and looked at me with bugged eyes. "I'm going to die!"

"Why?" It must be good. "What's in there?"

"*You,*" said Piper.

They opened the book up again, found the page, and slammed it shut again. They threw back their heads whiplash-like in laughter.

"Glad to see it's causing you so much amusement," I calmly said. "So, what'd I do?"

Apparently, I had "won" the honor of being the most searched Internet name—setting the world's record for most hits.

"Oh, hush." I rolled my eyes. The three look-alikes sounded like hyenas. "It could be worse."

Honestly, it freaked me out a bit. The 2008 presidential campaign had been a roller-coaster ride surrounded by all-things-circus some days. In both parties' camps, there were the political equivalent of jugglers, animals, clowns, puppeteers, and a few too many wannabe ringleaders. Now, back home in my living room with three giggling girls, it did feel a bit weird to have our little Christmas tradition infiltrated with a reminder of all the hoopla.

Eh, whatever . . . I guess that curiosity factor accounted for something. Sheesh.

It wasn't the worst thing that could've happened, but it did bring "real life" crashing into our lighthearted Christmas ritual. It's funny how many things have the ability to puncture our joy just a bit because we have such high expectations for the day. Not only does "real life" come in the form of tight budgets, short fuses, sketchy relationships, feelings of inadequacy after hearing how someone else more effectively captured the true spirit of Christmas, and even really bad salmon . . . canned back when Clinton was elected president. (No, the other Clinton.) And gas was barely a buck a gallon. It also comes when you just simply can't live up to the Folger's commercial.

Well, have no fear.

First, you're right. You won't "do Christmas" perfectly, and—chances are—things will go wrong in even your most gallant attempts to do it well.

Even after reading this you might respond too tersely to someone who wishes you "Happy holidays," instead of returning a nice, simple "Merry Christmas." Or, you might—because you have other battles in real life—not be able to utter a "Merry Christmas" at all.

Here's the good news the Christmas message whispers softly to you.

"Fear not."

That's what the angel said to Mary, and that's what God is saying to you now. As you wrangle through whatever challenges are going on in your life—financial distress, illness, concerns for your children or parents, even silly expectations you have about this season that rolls around again twelve months later anyway—it's natural for you to feel fear. But Christmas is not about the "natural," it's about the miraculous. Hebrews 2:14 says Jesus became man "that through death He might destroy him who has the power of death."

Isn't that a comforting thought, especially if Christ has taken away that nagging worst fear we all have in our hearts? The same fear I felt during "the great salmon scare" with my way-too-frugal dad?

Trials, hardships, and—yes—death are all part of our existence on earth. One day, I'll get the call and it won't be a comical false alarm and no one even likes thinking about it, but the message of Christmas resounds anyway.

Fear not.

Why?

God helpfully elaborates.

"For I am with you."

Be not dismayed.

Why?

"For I am your God."

It's so common to receive cards in the mail in December with Scripture verses on pretty paper in gold foil commemorating the season. But the words are more powerful than a decoration to tape around your door frames. Forget the dopey-hopey-changey things you hear from politicians promising an easier life if only you vote the way they tell you. The words of Scripture are the only words powerful enough to change your life and this culture.

"I will help you," God says. "I will strengthen you; I will uphold you with the right hand of My righteousness. . . . Do not be anxious about your life, what you shall eat or what you shall wear. . . . Cast all your anxieties on God because He cares for you. . . . The Lord is my light and my Salvation: whom shall I fear. The Lord is the stronghold of my life: of whom shall I be afraid?"

Christmas gently encourages you in your weakness.

You don't have to be perfect. Perfection came, wrapped in swaddling clothes and placed in a humble manger. His life and death free you from others' expectations, from cultural decay, and even from your own inadequacies.

That's why you can rest this season, because perfection doesn't depend on you. Ever wonder why there are so many candles during Christmas?

"In Him was life and the life was the light of men. The light shines in the darkness, and the darkness has not overcome it."

This year, truly accept the joy and peace the holiday offers.

It can change your life.

It's already changed the world.

Merry Christmas.

During Christmas Break in 2010, Todd, Bristol, Greta Van Susteren, and I traveled to Haiti with Reverend Franklin Graham's organization, Samaritan's Purse. One highlight was handing out Christmas gifts to precious, innocent orphans who could not survive without generous people like Greta or the Grahams.

Recipes

"Should we go?" I asked Todd one day over the phone. My husband was preparing to meet me in Colorado after a speech, but an invitation to a birthday party caused us to reevaluate our plans. The man having the birthday is a millionaire, or maybe he's a billionaire. I don't know, hundreds of millions here, hundreds of millions there . . . pretty soon we're talking real money. Though he's wealthy, you'd never know it if you just met him because he's grounded, unassuming, hardworking.

"It's a once-in-a-lifetime thing," Todd said. Attending the party meant we'd have to take a slight northern detour, so we'd have to adjust our plans. Since I'm always inspired to meet a fun group of successful entrepreneurs, we decided to go for it.

"Live life vibrantly," I said. Todd and I, over the course of our marriage, have really lived this mantra from the beginning of our relationship. Twenty-five years ago, we lived it out by not telling anyone that we were getting married, not overthinking the ceremony, and not incurring any debt. (Todd says that's why my dad loves him so much, because he had his first daughter married off for only thirty-five bucks!) We just independently knew it was right so we forged full-speed ahead. Later, we lived out this mantra when I decided to run against good ol' boy GOP incumbents for mayor, then governor, because I knew the public deserved new energy to get the job done. Then, we lived out this mantra by saying yes to the many adventures we've had commercial fishing together in Bristol Bay; traveling across the country on some crazy fun road trips to taste America's history; encouraging the kids to make sacrifices today and work hard and ignore the critics. I even have a handwritten sign on the kitchen cabinet that reads, "Do today what others won't, so you can do tomorrow what others want."

These are all examples of living that mantra, and it comes in handy when we have to decide whether to take the more convenient plan or the more adventurous route. We *always* take the more adventurous route.

"But wait," I said, realizing that we needed a gift if we were going to a birthday party. "What do you get someone who has everything?"

"I'm sure he doesn't need a gas card," Todd said.

"Or an ice auger," I said.

"There's got to be something truly unique," I thought.

"Since I'm still here," Todd offered, "I could grab something that's from Alaska."

Suddenly, I was inspired.

"Can you thief an oosik from my dad's garage?" Dad was notorious for his collection of antlers, fossils, petrified wood, and so many other things.

"Well, it's definitely . . ." he struggled for the right word, ". . . *authentic.*"

"Make sure you pack it carefully!" I said. I was worried the small, straight bone might be damaged in transport.

I went ahead and delivered my speech in Colorado and was excited to see Todd when he landed.

"Where's the oosik?"

"I was afraid TSA would confiscate it," Todd confessed. "So I didn't pack the bone."

Dang it! Now what would we bring?

"You're probably right," I muttered. We've never even gotten on a flight without TSA opening and testing and poking and sometimes even confiscating Trig's jars of puréed baby food.

"But now we won't have a unique gift."

I had a few hours before the party, so I went to a friend's house and asked her if I could use her oven. Then I texted my girlfriend Juanita and had her text me back for the umpteenth time her secret recipe for—I swear to you—the best oatmeal-raisin-white-chocolate-chip cookies in the world.

"Why do you keep losing it?" she texted back, before relenting and sending it to me again. After every time she sends it, she always adds, "Don't give it to anyone!"

I only had a few hours, but I used every one of them to bake these cookies. I also bought very festive, professional-looking bakery bags with silver ties. I can never bake them quite as well as Juanita—and it's always more fun with her in the kitchen *with* me—but these cookies turned out soft and gooey. I knew I had the perfect gift. Not only are they indisputably the most heavenly treats, but also I think cooking and baking for others is symbolic of how much they mean to you. You've spent your precious time on them, not on yourself. It also means you didn't point, click, and send directly from the online store—complete with the five-dollar gift wrapping.

Every year, I go to Carrs in Wasilla—our town's great grocery store—and buy the best ingredients for my Christmas concoctions. I love to give pots of home-made moose chili, tubs of scrumptious smoked salmon dip (made from wild salmon we caught), peanut butter balls sprinkled with the kids' handiwork, and Juanita's famous cookies for gifts every year.

Indicative of my family's highbrow foo-foo, chi-chi tastes, I told Willow I was including favorite recipes in this Christmas book and she insisted on her traditional favorite. No, not the warm baked brie with a cranberry base in a flaky crust, and not Heather's to-die-for, inch-thick, frosting-piled-high soft gingerbread men, and not Grandma Sally's beer-battered halibut I request every potluck. Instead, Willow claimed, "You can*not* write a book without including our Rice Krispies treats, Mom. It's not Christmas without them."

Sigh.

We went to the party and our friend in Colorado smiled when he opened the package and saw the gooey treats.

"This is deeply touching," he said, inhaling the sweet aroma. "Thank you."

It was a sweet moment, and I could tell he really appreciated the time and love that went into that batch of cookies. I'd rather have seen the look on his face after opening the oosik. It would have been even better to see his face after he googled the term to find out what it was! However, his sincere response to my homemade gift confirmed the lessons learned from Mom. Nothing says Christmas like strapping on an apron, heading to the kitchen with friends and family, and cooking and baking yourself into the Christmas spirit.

I hope you enjoy these special Palin recipes we've been loving for years.

Some have been passed down and around without exact measurements, and I'm passing them along to you the same way I received them.

That means you get to experiment a little to discover the perfect combination for your family. (And, by the way, I'm including that famous cookie recipe in this book for you to enjoy. . . . Just don't tell Juanita!)

Enjoy!

Sarah

Merry Christmoose Chili

I guarantee this will become a family favorite—not only for your guests, but for you, because it's so easy to make. Everyone loves it!

TIME TO PREPARE: *1 to 5 hours, depending on how long you want it to simmer in your Crock-Pot.*

SERVES: *I promise you this meal is so hearty and so good! The recipe as follows will serve eight, but just add more cans of kidney beans to the pot to keep up with the number of guests coming through your door. We usually have a Crock-Pot full on the counter all throughout the holidays.*

1 pound moose hamburger (or caribou or, heck, I suppose you can use beef)

1 package of regular chili seasoning mix

1 package of hot chili seasoning mix

Two 16-ounce cans of tomato sauce

Eight 16-ounce cans of kidney beans

1. Over a medium flame brown the meat in a large stovetop pan. Once it is browned, transfer the meat to a Crock-Pot if you are using one. Add the chili seasoning

mixes, tomato sauce, and kidney beans. (I drain about half the cans of beans, the rest I just pour in.)

2. Stir the chili, bring to a boil, and then simmer for at least one hour.

3. The toppings make the chili. We use shredded cheese and dollops of sour cream atop each bowl. I set out chopped onions as another option. Todd and the other guys in the family tend to go for Pilot Bread to dip into their chili. (It's also called Sailor Boy. It's a thick, round dry wafer that is one of our most versatile foods. You can spread peanut butter or Spam on it, and you'll find this staple in every tackle box or cooler up north. I don't believe these crackers *ever* expire.) Others prefer tortilla chips to sprinkle on top.

Rice Krispies Treats

In honor of Willow Bianca, I present the holiday's simplest classic. It might not be the fanciest Christmas recipe, but it's definitely one of the more delicious!

TIME TO PREPARE: *20 minutes*

YIELDS: *Twenty-four 2 x 2-inch squares, but you might want to cut them a little bigger. They are that good!*

3 tablespoons butter or margarine

1 package (approximately 40) marshmallows

6 cups Rice Krispies cereal

1. In a large pan on the stovetop melt the butter over low heat. Add the marshmallows and stir until it's a gooey white cloud of marshmallow.

2. Pour your Rice Krispies in the pan, remove from the heat, and stir well.

3. Using buttered fingers, press the cooled mixture into a buttered 13 x 9 x 2–inch pan. Add decorative candies on top, like red hots. You can even decorate them with tiny green frosting leaves to look like mistletoe and holly.

Smoked Salmon Spread

Everyone loves this, except Bristol, who—inexplicably—is the only Alaskan I know who does not like to eat our Bristol Bay–caught salmon.

TIME TO PREPARE: *30 minutes*

YIELDS: *1½ pints*

1 8-ounce can of salmon, preferably smoked (if not, add liquid smoke to the spread)

8 ounces cream cheese, softened

2 tablespoons onion, finely chopped

⅓ cup ranch dressing

½ teaspoon Worcestershire sauce

Tabasco, a dash, optional mayonnaise, optional, to taste jalapeños, diced, optional, to taste

1 tablespoon freshly squeezed lemon juice, optional

1. For the basic recipe, use a jar or can of salmon (preferably smoked) that you caught yourself. (Dad, if you are following this recipe, avoid salmon circa 1992!) In a large mixing bowl, combine the cream cheese with the onion (you can substitute onion powder). Add the ranch dressing—to make it more moist—a little Worcestershire

sauce, and a dash of Tabasco. If your salmon is not smoked, add the liquid smoke.

2. Really, you can't go wrong adding small amounts of other ingredients—like mayo, jalapeños, lemon juice—as long as you have that very basic, very perfect easy recipe as your base.

3. We also make this with halibut, and it doesn't have to be smoked. Mix mayonnaise with the cream cheese if you choose the halibut spread.

4. Spread on crackers, small squares of homemade bread, pita, or thinly sliced toasted bagels.

Heather's Gingerbread Cookies

"Just roll the dough thicker and underbake!"

Heather insists that's it—her deep, dark secret revealed to baking the season's best gingerbread men.

So perfect! Everyone asks Heather to bring these to parties. My siblings and I have birthdays all bunched together near the holidays, including Chuck and Heather—who are less than a year apart. Then I came along just barely twelve months later. So we have joint birthday potlucks, and thankfully gift giving is made easier now that I ask Heather to just make this cookie dough for my present. I freeze it, then roll it out for other shindigs.

It's a great gift!

She uses this adapted classic Betty Crocker recipe.

Note: Kids can cut the shapes. Frost generously.

TIME: *10 to 12 minutes*

YIELDS: *About 20 5-inch cookies*

Gingerbread People:

1½ cups dark molasses

1 cup packed brown sugar

⅔ cup cold water

⅓ cup shortening

7 cups all-purpose flour★

2 teaspoons baking soda

1 teaspoon salt

1 teaspoon ground allspice

2 teaspoons ground ginger

1 teaspoon ground cloves

1 teaspoon ground cinnamon

Heather's Frosting (see following page)

1. Preheat oven to 350°F.

2. In a large bowl, mix the molasses, brown sugar, water, and shortening.

3. Fold in the remaining ingredients except frosting. Cover and refrigerate the dough for at least two hours.

4. On a floured surface, roll the dough ¼-inch thick. Cut the dough with a floured gingerbread cutter or any other favorite shaped cutter you like.

5. Place the cookies about 2 inches apart on a cookie sheet sprayed with Pam or greased with butter.

6. Bake the cookies until no indentation remains when touched, about 8 minutes. Make sure you don't overbake them! Cool and decorate with Heather's Frosting (recipe follows).

NOTE: If you want to make gingerbread cookies instead of the people, then:

★ If using self-rising flour, omit the baking soda and salt.

Decrease flour to 6 cups. Roll dough ½ inch thick and cut with floured 2½-inch round cutter. Place about 1½ inches apart on lightly greased cookie sheet. Bake *less than* 15 minutes—remember to underbake them to get them soft.

Heather's Frosting:
4 cups powdered sugar
¼ cup shortening
¼ butter or margarine
1 teaspoon vanilla
1 teaspoon mint flavoring (optional, but tastes great on gingerbread men, especially, it seems, if you use green food coloring)
¼ cup milk

1. Mix on high speed, but you may need more or less milk, depending on the consistency you desire for your frosting. Be prepared to add a few drops until the frosting is soft enough to spread easily on top of the cookies—or add more powdered sugar if you need to thicken it up.

2. We scoop out some frosting and put it in separate bowls and add to these separate portions different colored drops of food coloring—usually using lots of green and red—depending on how you want to decorate your cookies.

3. We add red hots and sprinkles and tiny candies or anything else on top of a base of this simple, delicious frosting to create and decorate our gingerbread men!

Juanita's Soft, Gooey Oatmeal Raisin White Chocolate-Chip Heaven

Now, you can have the perfect gift to give your loved ones at Christmas! It's fun to give these away in festive packaging. These delicious little treats deserve it!

TIME TO PREPARE: *20 minutes*

YIELDS: *About 4 dozen cookies*

2 sticks semi-hard butter (still chilled from the fridge, *not* softened in the microwave, and don't overmix the butter with the sugars, eggs, and vanilla)

1 cup brown sugar

½ cup white sugar

2 eggs

1 teaspoon vanilla

1½ cup flour plus a smidge more

1 teaspoon baking soda plus a smidge more

½ teaspoon salt

1 teaspoon cinnamon and a few pinches of allspice

3 cups oatmeal

lots of white chocolate chips; Juanita adds some dark and semisweet chocolate chips, too.

raisins, to taste (or dried cranberries to make cookies more colorfully festive)

1 cup (or so) chopped walnuts unless your kids demand "no nuts!"

1. Preheat your oven to 350° F.

2. In a large mixing bowl, mix together the butter, brown sugar, white sugar, eggs, and vanilla. Add the flour, baking soda, and salt. Fold in the oatmeal, white chocolate chips, raisins, and walnuts. You can chill the cookie dough in the fridge before scooping it out with a medium-sized ice-cream scoop, but it's not necessary. Scoop the dough onto ungreased cookie sheets.

3. Bake for about only 8 minutes.

NOTE: The cookies *have* to be gooey soft, almost raw in the center. They'll harden a bit as they cool on the counter.

Peanut Butter Balls

No one can remember which homemade cookbook we found this in a few decades ago—it was one of those hand-written kids' cookbooks. We quit measuring ingredients back in the 1980s, so now we have a general feel for this recipe. Once you make a successful batch of these delicious treats, you won't go by a strict recipe, either. However, I'll include my best guesstimate of quantities to help you when you are picking up ingredients from the grocery store. Please feel free to experiment with the quantities on this recipe—it's truly hard to mess up a recipe like this one!

PREP TIME: *30 minutes*

YIELDS: *About 60 pieces, depending on how big you make them*

2 cups creamy peanut butter
2 to 2½ cups powdered
  sugar
¼ cup butter
splash vanilla

9 ounces chocolate
  chips
sprinkles, nuts, flavored
  chocolate chips for
  topping, to taste

1. Mix together the creamy peanut butter, powdered sugar, and butter in a big bowl. Then add a splash of the

vanilla. It's got to be thick enough to scoop out the dough and form balls, so experiment a little to get the right thickness. If it's not stiff enough, just add more sugar. Meanwhile, melt the chocolate chips in a bowl in the microwave. Form the dough into balls; however large or small you would like. Then dip the balls into the melted chocolate chips. You can get fancy and add paraffin to the melted chocolate to add shine, but I usually skip that step.

2. After the balls are coated in chocolate, we roll some of them in colorful sprinkles, nuts, and different-flavored chopped chocolate chips to fit the Christmas theme. But the classic combination of simple chocolate and peanut butter without a lot of embellishment tastes best to me.

3. You can save the decorations for the small boxes you'll put them in, and I assure you the recipient will just love the plain peanut butter balls.

4. These taste better than Reese's!

Faye's Blueberry Pie Recipe

In this recipe, my mother-in-law, Faye Irene Palin (affectionately called FIP by family), uses fresh, wild, hand-picked Alaskan blueberries. FIP bakes this perfect pie for holidays and every autumn at her rustic Crosswinds Lake cabin, but notes, "I just have to get to the blueberries before the bears do!"

Enjoy this pie with the flakiest, most delicious crust (there are two different crust variations below), from a lifelong classy Alaskan woman!

Note, in the recipe below the crust ingredients have been doubled from FIP's original version, so expect some leftover dough. Faye must be able to roll the dough out so delicately and thinly that she needs half the amount I do to cover the entire pie crust. Not me. I'm too clumsy and need more dough to patch the holes. I have to double the recipe just to fit my one pie. What to do with the leftover dough? We use it for what we call "kids' crust." We drizzle melted butter on it and sprinkle on some cinnamon and sugar before baking it in a small pie tin for the kids to enjoy.

PREP TIME: *1 hour*

YIELDS: *1 pie crust*

First Pie Crust Option:8- or 9-Inch One-Crust Pie or Baked Shell

2 cups plus 4 tablespoons flour (Measure by the dip-level method. Level off the measuring cup with a straight-edged tool, such as the back of a table knife)

1 teaspoon salt

⅔ cup vegetable oil

4 tablespoons cold water

Preheat oven to 425° F. In a large bowl, mix the flour and salt. Add the oil and mix with a fork until it starts to look like meal. Sprinkle the flour mixture with water and continue to mix with a fork. Gather the dough together and press into a ball. Roll the crust between two long strips of waxed paper. Place the dough, paper-side-up, in pie pan. Peel off the wax paper. Fill with the blueberry filling (below) and finish the pie crust edges. Bake for 35 to 45 minutes, or until crust is brown.

Second Pie Crust Option: 8- or 9-Inch Two-Crust Pie

3½ cups flour

2 teaspoons salt

1 cup vegetable oil

6 tablespoons cold water

1. Preheat oven to 425° F. In a large bowl, mix the flour and salt. Add the oil and mix with a fork until it starts to look like meal. Sprinkle the flour mixture with water and continue to mix with a fork. Gather the dough together and press into a ball. Divide the flour almost in half. Use the larger half for the pie's bottom. Roll the bottom portion of the dough between two long strips of waxed paper. Place the dough, paper-side-up, in pie pan. Peel off the wax paper. Fill with the blueberry filling (below) and trim the edges. Roll the top portion of the dough on waxed paper. Cut slips in middle. Place the dough over the filling. Trim the dough ½ inch beyond rim, fold under, seal and flute.

2. I find that by always being exact in my measurements, the consistency of the crust is good. When you roll the dough out between the wax paper sheets, you can roll the crust very thin. You just have to be patient when you peel back the wax paper when you put the crust on the pie.

Fresh Blueberry Pie Filling

9-inch pie	*8-inch pie*
1 to 1½ cups sugar	⅔ to 1 cup sugar
⅓ cup flour	¼ cup flour
½ teaspoon cinnamon	½ teaspoon cinnamon
4 cups fresh berries	3 cups fresh berries
1½ tablespoons butter	1 tablespoon butter

1. Wash and drain the berries. Pick them over and remove any stems and hulls. Use the smaller or larger amount of sugar according to your taste and the sweetness of the blueberries.

2. Mix the sugar, flour, and cinnamon. Fold in the berries. Pour the berry mixture into a pastry-lined pie pan. *Dot with butter.* (I do this with every fruit pie—no matter what kind—apple, rhubarb, cherry, strawberry). Cover with the top crust if using. Seal and flute. Bake for 35 to 45 minutes or until crust is brown and juice begins to bubble through slits in crust.

Acknowledgments

Thank you so very much, Nancy French. It was beyond joyful to work with you on this book! To Nancy's beautiful family—including precious Camille, Austin, and Naomi—thank you for sharing your mama with me. Nancy made it pleasant to tap gadgets at all hours across many time zones, penning rounds of legalese together while sharing bucketfuls of laughs along the way.

Thank you to all the good people at HarperCollins. Thanks especially to Jonathan Burnham, Kathy Schneider, Leah Wasielewski, Leah Carlson-Stanisic, and Robin Bilardello. Special thanks to that Greek goddess, Tina Andreadis, and to my editor, Amy Bendell. Your ideas, encouragement, and expertise made this great. I appreciate the faith you have in this project.

Thanks again to Robert Barnett for being the amazing, courageous, and sharp D.C. man that you are, representing a melting pot of characters within which I'm sure you've seen it all. But you still haven't seen home in Alaska, Bob, so let me take you there so you can kick it in the sticks.

Thank you to folks who still teach the hard and good lessons of life, the lessons that may no longer be popular but are vital to success. Keep teaching truth, teach kids the history of this exceptional country we love, and—always—teach them to stick to their guns.

A big, big thank-you to my friends and family, and our diverse extended family, for making the memories recollected on these pages, and many more not included this time. I smile when remembering wonder-filled holidays we've shared in some picture-perfect snowy settings. Many more are to come.

A big thank-you to Todd's group of "manly man" buddies, who keep us busy, entertained, grounded, and in stitches.

I want to thank my kids for putting up with chilly scavenger hunts and warm recipe experiments. For patiently accepting simple presents that probably weren't as cool as your friends', and for always, always making Christmas so bright, please know I wouldn't trade our time together for anything in the world. By the way, I love your hearts and your humor, and I honor your work ethic. And my biggest thanks go to Todd, who's forever been my best gift.

There is no way to adequately thank our Lord for giving us Christmas. We'll protect it as best we can, and ask His strength to assist in our weakness.

In this—and in everything—I give Him the glory.

About the Author

Sarah Palin has served as a mayor, governor, and oil and gas industry regulator, and was the GOP's first female vice-presidential candidate. She's a *New York Times* bestselling author, Fox News contributor, and national and international speaker, and has received numerous awards, including being named one of *Time*'s 100 Most Influential People in the World.

The Palin family lives in Alaska, where they fish commercially in Bristol Bay, and in the off-season they enjoy hunting, fishing, hiking, distance running, road trips, lots of kids' sports, and miles of snowmachining. Wintertime competition revolves around Todd Palin's Iron Dog snowmachine race, but Sarah is content to take a pass on that arduous 2,000-mile race across Alaska. Instead, she fuels the racers with her family-style home cooking, which includes recipes that have been passed down from generation to generation.